Twayne's United States Authors Series

Sylvia E. Bowman, *Editor*

INDIANA UNIVERSITY

Joel Barlow

JOEL BARLOW

By ARTHUR L. FORD

Lebanon Valley College

 193

Twayne Publishers, Inc. :: New York

For M. E.

Preface

Most criticism of eighteenth-century American literary figures, especially of the minor ones, concentrates on biography, historical frameworks, intellectual currents, religious and political backgrounds, and, occasionally, on esthetic values and literary tastes; but few actually discuss in any detail the works themselves. Perhaps it is unwise to examine these works too closely, or perhaps it is just unnecessary; most of them simply are not very well done. It is, however, equally unwise, I believe, to ignore them completely and to be satisfied with briefly talking about them.

Joel Barlow was unique among his associates in the gradual but dramatic shift which took place in his political, religious, and social ideologies. Between the publication of *The Vision of Columbus* in 1787 and his return to America in 1804, Barlow's orientation shifted from conservative Protestant-Federalist to Deistic-Jeffersonian; and in my examination, in Chapters 2 and 3, of *The Vision* and its later revisions, culminating in *The Columbiad* of 1807, I have attempted to trace this change and to show how it affected these poems. Chapter 4 examines in detail several of Barlow's shorter poems, two of which, "The Hasty Pudding" and "Advice to a Raven in Russia," contain some of the best poetry written by an American during this era; and Chapter 5 discusses Barlow's prose which reveals a skilled handler of the political plain style and a devout humanitarian.

Joel Barlow's political theme is America's future greatness, a theme which he shouts all too awkwardly and all too insistently in his poetry; but in his prose this theme radiates quite naturally from the mass of advice which he passed on to his contemporaries of several countries and to their descendants. This study discusses, therefore, Barlow's literary production within the matrix of his world; but it also focuses attention, especially in his shorter poems, on his effective use of form to underscore, and at times reveal, content.

In the course of this discussion, I have discovered several things. First, Barlow, as everyone might suspect, produced relatively little of lasting value—but more than most critics acknowledge and more in his prose than in his better known poetry. Second, I found it impossible to avoid the man and his age. Even after presumably disposing of both in the first chapter, I found myself returning with admiration to the humanity of Barlow's statements and with fascination to the political-historical-sociological events that swirled around him throughout his life. It is, of course, impossible to understand *The Vision of Columbus* or *Advice to the Privileged Orders* outside this biographical-historical frame, but I have attempted to keep it subordinate to the examination of Barlow's prose and poetry.

Joel Barlow is fortunate to have a biographer such as James Woodress, and the Connecticut Wits are fortunate to have a scholar such as Leon Howard. I have relied upon them, as well as upon the earlier biographies by Theodore Zunder and Charles Burr Todd, for many of the details of Barlow's life. Thanks is also due J. Robert Bashore of Bowling Green State University who first introduced me to Joel Barlow and his friends, to Lebanon Valley College for a Faculty Research Grant which aided me in collecting material, and to Joel Barlow of Washington, D. C., who provided me with a copy of the Charles Wilson Peale portrait of his ancestor. Finally, I would like to thank the librarians and staffs of the following libraries for their graciousness and thoughtfulness: The Lebanon Valley College Library, The Franklin and Marshall College Library, The Yale University Library, The Harvard University Library, The Rutherford B. Hayes Library, and the Library of Congress. Certain unpublished materials are quoted by permission of the Harvard College Library and the Yale University Library.

ARTHUR L. FORD

Lebanon Valley College

Contents

Chapter

Preface

Chronology

1.   Connecticut Wit Transformed   13

2.   *The Vision of Columbus*   46

3.   Vision and Revision   68

4.   Poet of Corn-Meal Mush   85

5.   The Vision of Joel Barlow   107

6.   The Largeness of the Man   126

Notes and References   131

Selected Bibliography   135

Index   142

Chronology

1764   Joel Barlow born March 24, 1754, in a Redding, Connecticut, farmhouse.

1774   Enrolled at Yale College.

1776   Spent summer with the Revolutionary Army.

1778   Graduated from Yale with bachelor of arts degree; as class poet, read "The Prospect of Peace."

1780-   Chaplain in the Revolutionary Army.
1782

1781   Married Ruth Baldwin.

1784   Founded, with Elisha Babcock, *The American Mercury*; partnership dissolved in 1785.

1786   Admitted to the bar.

1787   *The Vision of Columbus.*

1788   Left for Europe to sell land for the Ohio Company.

1790-   Lived in England.
1792

1792   *Advice to the Privileged Orders*; "The Conspiracy of Kings"; *A Letter to the National Convention.*

1793   Campaigned unsuccessfully for election to the National Assembly; *A Letter to the People of Piedmont*; "The Hasty Pudding."

1796-   United States consul to Algiers.
1797

1799   *Letters from Paris.*

1804   Returned to America.

1806   *Prospectus of a National Institution.*

1807   *The Columbiad.*

1811   Appointed minister to France.

1812   Joel Barlow died of pneumonia in Zarnowiec, near Cracow, Poland, while caught in Napoleon's retreat from Russia. He had been attempting to conclude a treaty with Napoleon.

CHAPTER 1

Connecticut Wit Transformed

IN A LETTER to Oliver Wolcott, a friend, Joel Barlow said, "I am determined to love mankind if they kill me." In a sense, this statement, made only in half-seriousness, serves as a summary of Barlow's life and career. One of many citizens of the young republic to devote his life to his country and its people, Joel Barlow died in Poland during the incredibly devastating retreat of Napoleon's army from Russia in 1812. Before his death, however, he had built several reputations and many careers. Publisher, chaplain, international businessman, pamphleteer, diplomat, statesman, financier of inventions, adviser to presidents, liberal thinker, and epic poet of America, Barlow was directly and indirectly involved in most of the significant events of his time; and, in addition, he earned the reputation of being at the time America's foremost poet. Succeeding generations were to see faults in his poetry that admirers were blinded to in his lifetime, but in a period that had little time for *belles lettres* and produced little imaginative literature of lasting importance, Joel Barlow held a place of esteem and honor. In a period of intense nationalism, Barlow reflected the spirit of his times by dedicating his poetry, like his life, to the future glory of America and mankind.

I *Writer Apprentice*

Joel Barlow was born March 24, 1754, in a clapboard farmhouse in Redding, Connecticut.[1] His father, Samuel Barlow, farmed the land; and Joel, next to the youngest of nine children, grew up among the Connecticut hills, performed the farm chores that might be expected of any young boy and attended the village school. At the age of nineteen, he studied at Moor's Indian School at Hanover, New Hampshire, a preparatory school for Dartmouth College; and the next year he enrolled at Dartmouth. Three months later, however, following his father's death, Joel decided to use his small inheritance to seek a better school in a more urban environment; and so, in 1774, less than a year before the Battle of Lexington and Concord, Joel Barlow, an inexperienced farm boy, entered the sophisticated life of Yale University at New Haven.

The college at this time was well respected, but it was also known for its conservatism, especially in religion. As Leon Howard describes it, "It was a highly specialized institution in which students acquired the conventional points of view and basic assumptions necessary for communication with a public that had little time and less desire for novelty in thought and literature."[2] The two great virtues of its graduates were piety and practicality—with one wholly dependent on the other; and the ideal Yale graduate was the one who caused the least ruffle on the placid surface of New Haven society. Barlow's biographer, James Woodress, has reconstructed a typical undergraduate day: "rise at 5:30; attend prayers and recitation lasting till 7:30; study till 11; recite from 11 to 12; dine at 12; walk or take other exercise till 3; study again till 6; go to prayers and supper; spend evening in conversation; retire at 9."[3]

In general, the intellectual atmosphere was musty, and most of the work was dull. Independent study and thinking were discouraged; in fact, the second student law threatened expulsion for any heretical utterances. The religion textbook used by the college was Jonathan Edwards' *Inquiry Into the Freedom of the Will*, which was based on the strict orthodoxy of earlier Puritanism; and, for those students completely immersed in the college, the result was usually withering. For students such as Joel Barlow, who were interested in literature, a new concept of literary criticism was, however, being discussed.

The accepted function of poetry throughout colonial New England was to provide a vehicle for the expression of abstract truths, usually religious but sometimes political. The value of the poetry was measured by how well it corresponded to the doctrines of the church or of a particular political body. By 1770, however, a new work by the Scottish common-sense philosopher, Lord Kames, was well known among Yale undergraduates. His *Elements of Criticism* insisted that man was not naturally depraved, as the Puritans believed, but naturally disposed to good. Furthermore, it maintained that each man has a sense that he shares with all men (common sense) which tells him what is good in human nature and also in the arts. Therefore, that which men naturally agree to be good is good; and literature which men of the Enlightenment believe to be esthetically pleasing is good.[4] This attitude, little more than the combination of Rousseau's noble savage and the eighteenth-century idea of uniformitarianism, opposed almost completely the Puritan insistence on man's natural lack of insight; and the concept was, in New England, radical—if not heretical—when Joel Barlow discovered it in 1774.

Although Barlow later developed into a religiously and politically liberal thinker, alienating many of his college friends, he remained while at Yale a reasonably orthodox New Englander. It was at Yale, however, that Barlow met Joseph Buckminster, the new tutor to the freshman class, who encouraged him in his poetic attempts and continued to give advice on a variety of subjects, including poetry, after they had both left Yale. In a letter dated January 11, 1779, Reverend Buckminster urged Barlow to consider a life in the ministry; and then he gave a frank estimate of the public attitude toward poets: "But you must remember that neither our country nor our Country men are sufficiently refined inriched [*sic*] and improved to give a sufficient support to works of Genius, merely and had you the genius of a Pope or a Milton nay as much superior as you wish might starve upon the pittance that a few Persons capable of relishing your productions would give. . . ."[5]

A few months later, Buckminster ended a letter with some advice concerning liberal attitudes toward religion: "But my Dear sir Whether you enter the ministry or not proceed in religion, and let your religion be rational derived from the Scriptures, and not formed from any human Creeds or Homilies but judge and examine for yourself for we stand or fall to our own Master. . . ."[6] Apparently, Yale had not succeeded completely in keeping unorthodox opinions away from its students.

In spite of Barlow's personal losses, his mother's and his brother's deaths, and despite the excitement and distraction of war, Barlow returned to college for his sophomore year and began to write poetry. Although he became known among the student body for his poetry and was apparently encouraged in it, only a few poems remain of these years; and they show that Barlow had been reading the poetry of seventeenth- and early eighteenth-century England. The following poem suggests the Cavalier poetry of the previous century:

> Go Rose my Chloe's bosom grace
> How happy should I prove
> Might I supply that env'd place
> With never fading love
> There Phoenix like beneath her eye
> Involved in fragrance burn & die
> * * *
> Know hapless flowers that thou shalt find
> More fragrant roses there
> I see thy withering head reclin'd
> With envy & despair
> One common fate we both must prove
> You die with envy and I with love.[7]

Another poem which Barlow wrote during his college years described a snowball fight between the freshmen and the sophomores. Although the poem no longer exists, the prose summary of it suggests Barlow's use of a mock-heroic form, including the intervention of the gods. The influence of Pope is obvious, and the poem revealed Barlow's wit and good humor; it established him as a poet of considerable popularity on the Yale campus.

The year was 1776, and the combination of the Declaration of Independence and the growing momentum of the British army caused most of the young men at Yale, including Joel Barlow, to march off to help General Washington at the Battle of Long Island. After participating in a two-month combination of defeat and retreat, Barlow returned to New Haven in August for the beginning of his junior year; he was not to return to battle for four years. Barlow's last two undergraduate years at Yale were marked by the near collapse of the college, by the dispersal of the student body to several nearby towns, by student uprisings against college policy and procedures (including college food), and, finally, by the resignation of the much-attacked president, Naphtali Daggett. Barlow undoubtedly hastened this resignation and assured his place as class poet when he wrote a parody of the Book of Chronicles in December, 1776:

1. And it came to pass on the third day of the tenth month, that there went forth a decree from Naphtali, the son of Zebulon, that all the captives throughout his dominion should depart for a little season, into the land of their nativity, to buy themselves some bread.

2. For it was so, that in the days of Naphtali, there was no bread in all the country round about, insomuch that there was a famine throughout the land of Naphtali.

3. Now Naphtali was a great man and ate much bread, insomuch that the famine was very sore.

4. Moreover, there were beans in great abundance in that land; so that Naphtali said, peradventure my captives that are in this land will eat beans thereof.

5. Howbeit, the captives were not accustomed to eat beans in their country; therefore they murmured against the hand of their master, saying give us bread to eat.

6. Wherefore Naphtali assembled all the sons of his captivity, and lifted up his voice in the midst of them, and said, O ye sons of my captivity, hear ye the words of Naphtali.

7. Forasmuch as the famine is sore in the land, insomuch there is hardly bread enough for me and my household:

8. Wherefore ye sons of the captivity of Naphtali, behold you may return to your houses in the land of your nativity, where ye can get some bread, lest ye die.

9. Nevertheless, when you shall hear the voice of my decree in the land of your fathers, saying unto you, return into the land of Naphtali.

10. Then it shall come to pass, that ye shall return and sojourn again in the land of captivity.

11. Thus was it done according to all the words of Naphtali.[8]

Barlow's senior year amounted to only two months of instruction because of the reduction of the regular school year to four months and because of a two-month absence by Barlow and four other students to protest actions taken by the college corporation concerning housing.

On July 23, 1778, Yale College held its senior exercises which contained, among examinations and declamations, the reading of a patriotic poem by the class poet, Joel Barlow. "The Prospect of Peace," an undistinguished piece in heroic couplets, is important primarily because it expressed ideas which Barlow used later in his more ambitious work, *The Vision of Columbus*, including praise of America's struggle for freedom and her future greatness. The poem was received well by the enthusiastic but generally uncritical audience, and it was immediately published in pamphlet form by a local printer. Joseph Buckminster, replying to a copy of the poem sent to him by Barlow, said, "I advise you to encourage and cultivate your turn for poetry."[9] The patriotic fervor of the poem undoubtedly aided in its favorable reception as did the Calvinistic sentiments with which it ended:

> THEN Love shall rule, and Innocence adore,
> Discord shall cease, and Tyrants be no more;
> 'Till yon bright orb, and those celestial spheres,
> In radiant circles, mark a thousand years;
> 'Till the grand *fiat* burst th'etherial frames;
> Worlds crush on worlds, and Nature sink in flames!
> The Church elect, from smouldering ruins, rise,
> And sail triumphant thro' the yielding skies,
> Hail'd by the Bridegroom! to the Father given,
> The Joy of Angels, and the Queen of Heaven! (11–12)

When Joel Barlow was graduated from Yale in 1778, he was a changed young man in many ways. Now an urbanized scholar and poet rather than the bewildered farm boy who had entered four years previously, he also differed from many of his fellow classmates, who constituted one of the great classes in Yale's history. Noah Webster, Oliver Wolcott, Josiah Meigs, in addition to others from earlier classes, including Timothy Dwight and John Trumbull, retained their staunch Calvinism throughout their lives; but Joel Barlow was soon to adopt political and religious beliefs totally alien to those commonly held at Yale. It is a mistake to assume that his Jeffersonianism and Deism were products solely of his later years, for it was at Yale that he revealed an independent and inquiring mind that was not satisfied with established opinion; and, ironically, it was a Yale teacher and minister, Joseph Buckminster, who introduced him to the many different avenues to truth and salvation.

II   *Pursuit of a Vision*

Following a winter of teaching school in New Haven, and hating it, Barlow returned to Yale to work for a master's degree and to fulfill the poetic expectations of his friends. Full of ambition and confidence, he outlined and began an epic poem about the adventures of Cyrus the Great. Soon, however, he changed his mind and considered instead other epics about Daniel, Joseph, and Cain and Abel, as suggested by Buckminster. Finally, in March, 1779, Barlow wrote to Buckminster about the possibility of using America itself as a subject for an epic; and, by April, he had finished a detailed plan of what was to become his long, philosophical poem which brought him national recognition, *The Vision of Columbus.*

A year of work on his poem had exhausted his supply of money, and no immediate support seemed forthcoming in spite of vigorous effort on the part of his friends; so, in the spring of 1780, Barlow decided to take the advice of a friend, Colonel David Humphreys, and become a chaplain in the army. His light duties would allow him plenty of time for his poetry, and the pay was acceptable. All he needed was a license to preach, and he easily obtained one.

Barlow's performance as chaplain for the Third Massachusetts Brigade soon won him the attention of his superior officers, including General Washington, who invited Parson Barlow to dinner shortly after his vigorous sermon about patriotism, one occasioned by the betrayal of Benedict Arnold. In a letter to Ruth Baldwin, later to become Mrs. Barlow, Joel referred to his hero of *The Vision of Columbus* and *The Columbiad* as "the greatest man upon earth."[10] In other ways, his chaplaincy was very agreeable; his work, as anticipated, occupied only a small portion of his time; he was able to compose approximately six thousand lines of his *Vision*; he enjoyed many evenings of conversation with the officers; and he continued to have the support and encouragement of Colonel Humphreys in the composition of his poetry. Humphreys, later coupled with Barlow by literary historians as one of the Connecticut Wits, spent a good deal of his time writing to friends trying to enlist support for Barlow's poem.

During the winter months a Revolutionary chaplain was not expected to be with his troops, so Barlow left for New Haven on October 29, 1780, to be reunited with "the worthiest girl that ever blest an honest heart,"[11] Ruth Baldwin, sister of Barlow's former roommate and good friend, Abraham Baldwin. More confident of his future than was Ruth's father, Barlow married Ruth in secrecy on January 26, 1781. Michael Baldwin was not to know of his daughter's marriage for more than a year, after which Barlow wrote the following to his father-in-law: "From my first acquaintance with your daughter she appeared to me the only person that could make me happy; my situation in life, as it appeared to others, was then unpromising . . . and I was repeatedly told that the connection would be disagreeable to you. . . . To crowd himself into a family is what no Gentleman of my feelings ever will do; but to take a daughter from any family upon the principle of mutual affection is a right always given by the God of nature wherever he has given that affection . . . we have been married more than a year. My affairs are now in good situation; I think they will enable me to maintain a family."[12] Few marriages have been happier, and some of Barlow's best prose can be found in letters written to Ruth during times of separation.

By the end of 1782, Joel was out of the army; and the Barlows had established residence in Hartford, the capital of Connecticut and one of the cultural centers of the young country. Many of Barlow's friends lived there, including his old classmate, Noah Webster, and the poet, John Trumbull, who completed the group of four poets later referred to as the Connecticut Wits. Barlow had taught and written at Timothy Dwight's school in Northampton, David Humphreys had been a good friend in the army, and now John Trumbull lived in the same town. During this time, Barlow was full of confidence; he had already finished over four-fifths of his *Vision*, he was busy rewriting and revising, and he was receiving substantial, though uncritical, encouragement from his friends. Monetary encouragement, however, was a little more difficult to come by. During the fall of 1782, Barlow toured several of the states trying to build a subscription list which would cover the cost of publishing his poem. Despite initial support, Barlow was unable to complete his poem before his funds ran out, causing him to search for other sources of income.

A happy solution appeared in 1784 when Barlow combined with Elisha Babcock, a printer from Springfield, to publish on the morning of July 12, *The American Mercury*, a weekly newspaper which enjoyed early and lasting success. Barlow did most of the writing for the paper—all of it representative of the turgid style and occasional verse of the period's newspapers. The venture, however, also gave the publishers an opportunity to enter into book publishing; and during 1785, the firm published an almanac, always a certain seller; a textbook by Barlow's friend, Noah Webster, containing several selections from the unpublished *Vision*; and an edition of *Watts's Psalms.* The new edition of the *Psalms* was Barlow's project, but it was encouraged by the ministerial association, and it was also prompted by the patriotic fervor of the period. Barlow brought the Psalms more into line with New England Protestantism, and he excised Watts's many references to the English monarchy. The new edition was not particularly noteworthy, although Barlow did poetize several of the Psalms ignored by Watts.

Although the reputation of *The American Mercury* and the firm of Barlow and Babcock grew steadily, the financial growth was less satisfactory. Because the business could support only one owner, the partnership was dissolved; and on December 5, 1785, the following notice appeared on the front page of the *American Mercury*:

JOEL BARLOW & ELISHA BABCOCK

HAVING by mutual consent dissolved their partnership, request all those who have accounts open with the late firm of BARLOW & BABCOCK to forward them for settlement as soon as convenient. Those who are indebted to them may depend on having their payment made easy provided it be made soon.

Said BABCOCK will carry on the Printing business, and endeavor to please every body.

Said BARLOW has opened a store of BOOKS, and other Goods at the house of the late Doctor Jepson near the South Meeting House; where may be had the new Edition of Psalms and Hymns. . . .

LIKEWISE

Rum, Sugar, Molasses, Hyson and Bohea Teas, Alspcie, [*sic*] Ginger, Broad Cloths, Coatings, Gamblets, Chintzes, Callicoes, Gauzes, Ribons &c.—
Any kind of Public Securities or Country Produce taken in Payment.

One of Barlow's careers had closed, and another was about to begin.

Barlow had also decided that he could support himself handsomely by going into law, and so he began to prepare himself for his bar examination; and in April, 1786, he was admitted to the bar. Barlow's dissertation was logical and competent; but, more important, it revealed ideas that were later to place him in the camp of radical thinkers and were to alienate many of his closest friends. Natural laws and societal laws, Barlow maintained, were both God-given and subject to growth and evolution. To the staunch conservative of New England, who supported the status quo, this idea was heresy when it was later revealed to a larger audience and in more violent terms. For the present, however, it attracted little attention—as did Barlow the lawyer. Barlow's law practice led him, within two years, directly to Paris and to the major turning point in his career, but before this event occurred, two important volumes were published: *The Anarchiad* in twelve installments from October 26, 1786, to September 13, 1787, in *The New Haven Gazette and Connecticut Magazine*; and *The Vision of Columbus* on May 14, 1787.

The Anarchiad was the product of four men who decided to collaborate on a satire which would allow them to express their opinions about a variety of subjects, including Shays's Rebellion and paper money. The authors were Joel Barlow, David Humphreys, John Trumbull, and Dr. Lemuel Hopkins, although which portions were written by which authors is impossible to determine. Nothing about *The Anarchiad* was very original; however, it did spark its share of political discussion. The work had as its models any number of satires in print at this time, including *The Rolliad*, a current English satire, and, earlier, Pope's *The Dunciad*. In the conclusion to the first number the authors made a witty jab at their poetic inspiration: "I know not whether it is necessary to remark, in this place, what the critical reader will probably have already observed, that the celebrated English poet, Mr. Pope, has proven himself a noted plagiarist, by copying the preceding ideas, and even couplets almost entire, into the famous poem called 'The Dunciad.' " The framework was simple and often used. An archeological expedition to the Muskingum River in Ohio discovered the remains of a prehistoric civilization; and among the ruins was found a manuscript of an epic poem, *The Anarchiad, A Poem, on the Restoration of Chaos and Substantial Night, in Twenty Four Books.*

The Anarchiad was presented during a turbulent time in American history. To the respectable and orderly New Englander, the country appeared to be descending into lawlessness and confusion. The rebellion of Daniel Shays brought the country close to complete anarchy; the introduction of paper money threatened to undermine and destroy the shaky foundation of the new country. In response to this situation, the poem emphasized the necessity of a strong, federal government, expressed a desire for order and stability at the expense of individual action, and revealed a preoccupation with nationalistic pride, all of which were Federalist attitudes.

Luther G. Riggs resurrected *The Anarchiad* in book form at another time, 1861, when the country's unity was being threatened. In his preface, Riggs said that the poem "tended in no small degree to check the leaders of insubordination and infidel philosophy."[13] Actually, the poem produced few political results. Politicians ridiculed by the authors were reelected to office, and the Great Debate between a strong, central government and a loose confederation of states continued for years to come.

As entertaining literature, however, the poem was quite successful and was enjoyed and discussed by many people in New England. The four men, together with Timothy Dwight, were quickly grouped as the "Wicked Wits," the "Hartford Wits," and, finally, as subsequent generations were to know them, the "Connecticut Wits." The Connecticut Wits never founded a club or thought of themselves as an organization in any sense. Rather, they are grouped together because of their close geographical proximity and because of the ideas they held in common. In religion, they were Calvinistic and reactionary, generally distrusting the liberal creed of Deism, which was fashionable among many intellectual and political leaders of the day. In politics, they were Federalistic and nationalistic, rejecting anything that was not native American and believing fervently in the future greatness of the young Republic.

In literature, they were nationalistic and imitative, a strange mixture that did not disturb them at all. As writers, they shouted feverishly, on one hand, for the establishment of a literary independence to parallel the political independence they had achieved. On the other hand, they slavishly imitated the heroic couplets of Alexander Pope, the balanced prose of Addison and Steele, and the satire of Jonathan Swift. The result was a great quantity of third- and fourth-rate Neoclassic verse having as its subject matter the coming glory of America. Although still included in anthologies, the Connecticut Wits have been relegated by later generations of literary historians to the distant background of American literature; however, in their day, they were immensely popular and constituted the first serious group of writers that America produced.

One of the ironies of American literature is that Joel Barlow, denounced in his later years as an atheist and anarchist, is known today chiefly as a member of the Connecticut Wits. Significant changes took place in his religious and political thinking, but he always retained, as did the other Wits, an intense desire to help found a native American literature, to give to America a usable literary tradition; and, in this effort, Barlow is simply one of a long line of writers, beginning well before the Revolution and extending into our century, who fought against a sense of inferiority with blatant cries of equality.[14] It is one thing to write a *Declaration of Independence*; it is quite another to write Walt Whitman's *Leaves of Grass.* Barlow's efforts at this time are symptomatic of the weaknesses in American literature in general. Political events necessitated a literature that subordinated esthetic values to more practical considerations, for the republic and its future were too important to ignore. Leon Howard, writing of The Connecticut Wits' achievement, says quite correctly that ". . . Their industry was directed toward quantity rather than quality: if they sweat at all, it was over mass production, not in casting to write a living line, for literature was a means to an end or an ornament upon an active life, not a life in itself. . . ."[15] And the truth remains that America during this time did not produce a writer great enough to transcend this provincialism.

While citizens were still discussing the jabs of *The Anarchiad*, Barlow finally managed to publish his long-delayed *The Vision of Columbus.* The subscribers had been waiting patiently and the public expectantly when on January 8, 1787, the *Connecticut Courant* ran the following advertisement:

Proposals for printing by Subscription, the

VISION OF COLUMBUS;

A POEM in Nine Books by Joel Barlow.
(Dedicated, by permission, to the KING OF FRANCE.)

THIS Work is now in the Press, at the Printing-Office of HUDSON and GOODWIN, and will be finished in about six weeks. It will be bound, gilt and lettered by an Artist equal to any in America, and perhaps not inferior to any workman in London.

It will be contained in one Volume, Octavo, and delivered to Subscribers at the price of ONE DOLLAR and a THIRD: A Price not higher than imported Books, of this size have commonly borne in America.

A list of Subscribers names will be printed at the end of the Volume.

Subscriptions taken in at this Office.

Hartford, January 1, 1787.

Praise was lavish even before the poem was published. In an article appearing in the *New-Haven Gazette* for February 1, 1787, the anonymous author discussed the forthcoming production and then made "an appeal to the bar of *critical taste*, to decide whether the writings of the Poets now living in Connecticut, are not equal to any which the present age can produce in the English language."[16] The year before, David Humphreys put it more simply: "Another Bard in conscious genius bold, / Now sings the new world happier than the old."[17]

The poem was dedicated to "His Most Christian Majesty, Louis the Sixteenth, King of France and Navarre," who generously bought twenty-five copies. Other subscribers, seven hundred and sixty-nine in all listed in an appendix, included George Washington, Benjamin Franklin, Thomas Paine, General Lafayette, Alexander Hamilton, and many other Revolutionary heroes and soldiers. The list prompted Leon Howard to remark that this "was their greatest exhibition of patriotism since the siege at Yorktown."[18] The poem was an initial, though not a lasting, financial success. Although no record exists of how many people actually read the poem, a second edition was in demand within a few months. James Woodress, Barlow's biographer, summed up the commercial success of the volume this way: "All things considered, the poem was in a modest way the first American best seller after the Revolution, and Barlow probably was the first American writer to receive fair pay for a book."[19] The poem, to be discussed later in more detail, makes use of the traditional vision technique, which allowed the author to expound on a variety of subjects connected with America's past, present, and future.

As might be expected, critical response to the poem was generally favorable, emphasizing the patriotic theme. An anonymous review in the *American Mercury*, Barlow's old newspaper, was flattering: "Mr. Barlow appears to be a natural poet, and to write with great ease and elegance; his style is pure and perspicuous; his numbers smooth and harmonious, equal, if not beyond, anything I ever read. His images are bright, striking, and often sublime; his painting is vivid and glowing; and the whole poem is full of fire and animation. . . ."[20] A letter written from Charles Kibly in England to Elias Shipman in 1788, now in the Yale Library, reflected the esteem in which the noncritical public held Barlow: "Barlow the Poet Laureate of all America is here, and is well spoke of—."

Most surprising of all was the publication, within a year, of *The Vision of Columbus* in England. The poem had been dedicated to the King of France, and it had recounted the heroic struggle of the colonies against the oppressions of a rather weak-minded British Empire. And yet, in response to the urgings of Barlow's friends and the quick reputation that the poem had won, *The Vision of Columbus* was published in England, without the dedication, during October, 1787. The English reviews were fair although, understandably, without the enthusiasm of many of the American reviews. One English review described the content, excused the excessive patriotism, and said simply, "Mr. Barlow thinks with freedom, and expresses himself with spirit."[21]

But man does not live by praise alone, and the revenue from the poem was dwindling rapidly. Joel Barlow discovered what many other people have recognized since then: to be a poet in

America, one must do other things to earn a living; and Barlow was a lawyer as well as a famous poet.

III *World Citizen*

Both these vocations made him a perfect candidate for a position that was to expose him to conditions which changed his life. Since the war, the westward migration of the continent had accelerated; and it was clear to all that money could be made by buying huge tracts of land from the government and then selling smaller lots to individuals or groups. One of the many companies formed for this purpose was the Ohio Company, composed mainly of Revolutionary War veterans who held bounty rights and Continental currency, which were practically worthless except in exchange for land. Through much, apparently legal, political manipulation, the Ohio Company, in connection with a shady group known as the Scioto Associates, managed to obtain five million acres of land in the Ohio River valley. One of the persons chosen to dispose of the land was Joel Barlow, who sold over one hundred and thirteen thousand acres in the first few months; and when Scioto Associates decided that the best source of revenue was Europe, Barlow was chosen to represent the firm. Excited by the prospect of traveling through Europe and by the prospect of helping America fulfill its destiny by populating the land, Barlow sailed alone for Europe on May 25, 1788. Although he expected to be gone only a short time, seventeen years passed before a very different Joel Barlow reentered the port of New York.

After a torturous journey, Barlow arrived in France and set out immediately for Paris, where he renewed his friendship with General Lafayette, met Thomas Jefferson, who was to be a lifelong friend, and became acquainted with a number of important Frenchmen and Americans. He spent a good bit of time sightseeing, and he made a trip to England where he talked with Thomas Paine and visited Twinkenham, the home of Alexander Pope, whose couplets Barlow tried heroically to emulate throughout his life. Barlow's business affairs were moving slowly; however, this fact did not seem to disturb him or keep him from enjoying the European countryside and its soci-

ety. His chief objective was to sell thousand-dollar shares of the
company, worth one thousand acres each, to European banks,
who would in turn sell them to individuals. The banks, however,
were unwilling to take a chance on the shares because Scioto Associates only held an option on the land and not the title to it.

A year after his arrival in Europe, Barlow had sold no shares;
but he was becoming involved in the political affairs of the decaying European powers, particularly of France. He rejoiced at
the Fall of the Bastille on July 14, 1789, giving thanks that he
could witness a second fight for freedom. Part pragmatist that
he was, he saw that those fleeing the revolution might be interested in emigrating to the New World; and he hurriedly set up
La Compagnie du Scioto to sell lots to individuals rather than
shares to banks. Although he had had no instructions to the
contrary, Barlow found Scioto Associates uninterested in his
new procedure, which would increase the flow of immigrants
but also reduce the profit to the company. As the first boat-
load of Frenchmen crossed the ocean in January, 1790, the
company began to wonder what it was going to do with them.

In Europe, Barlow's credit had gone bad; and the whole
company was gradually disintegrating. The word circulated
that the Scioto Company had no money, causing the purchasers
of the stock to stop payment. The settlement of the trans-
planted Frenchmen was equally disastrous; for inept subordi-
nates were designated to lead them into the Indian-infested
forests, to settle them on land that neither they nor the company owned, and to get them started farming the land, a task no
one was equipped to direct. Understandably, the Frenchmen
who arrived were bitter; their letters home were not the sort
that would bolster the company's reputation, as Barlow had
hoped.

Three years after Barlow had set out with hopes of making
his fortune, he was in debt, miserable, and threatened with
assassination by the distraught relatives and friends of the emi-
grants. His only fault had been a naïve trust of unscrupulous
men. It was an expensive lesson, but it was one Barlow was to
profit from later in his career. The last year of Barlow's unfortunate experience was lightened by the arrival of his wife, Ruth,
in July, 1790. They had missed each other terribly, and her

presence surely made the misery and embarrassment of his company's collapse endurable. Ruth was a devoted wife; and, despite her early displeasure with Europe, she managed to develop a fondness for it over the next fourteen years.

When Joel and Ruth were finally reunited, historic struggles were underway in the capitals of most European countries, especially in France and England. In France, Louis XVI was being held prisoner, and a new constitution had been delivered to the French people; in England, a debate raged over the necessity of revolution in Europe. The sides were clearly drawn, and Barlow was clearly on the side of the revolutionaries. Having participated in the glorious revolution of his own country and having seen it duplicated, or so he thought then, in France, he was convinced that the decaying monarchial systems of Europe must fall; and he determined to participate in this enlightened movement.

Arriving in England in 1790 for a stay that extended over two years, Barlow found himself in the midst of the liberal pro-French Revolution and anti-Burke group. Thomas Paine, Richard Price, Mary Wollstonecraft, Joseph Priestley, and Joseph Johnson eventually gave Barlow lessons in radicalism and made him receptive to liberal ideas in both politics and religion. Coming from the American Revolution, it is easy to see why Barlow inclined toward this group; the extent to which he adopted their extreme positions, however, was to alienate him from many of his old Yale friends. Already Barlow had come a long way from *The Anarchiad*, but he had a longer way to go.

Edmund Burke's 1790 attack on the French Revolution, *Reflections on the Revolution in France*, instantly produced scores of vigorous replies; the most famous, of course, and the most successful, was Paine's *Rights of Man.* Leading the many attacks of lesser significance was Barlow's reply, *Advice to the Privileged Orders in the Several States of Europe Resulting from the Necessity and Propriety of a General Revolution in the Principles of Government*, published February 4, 1792. An American giving advice to the privileged orders of Europe might have seemed a bit presumptuous to an European, but to an American it was the most logical thing in the world to do. After all, his people had already proven that a superior type of govern-

ment based on republican principles could work and benefit
the people, a view earlier expressed in *The Vision of Columbus.*
Advice to the Privileged Orders, though not so famous as
Paine's pamphlet, was effective enough to create a stir in the
English Parliament; and, until the recent publication of his
works, it was Barlow's only work still in print and was easily
accessible to the general reader.[22] Woodress believes this pamphlet to be his "most important and lasting work."[23]

Barlow, now a full-fledged radical, was elected to member-
ship in the Constitution Society, one of the many societies in
England created to champion the cause of the French Revolution and to urge changes within the English government. During
this time, Barlow published, also in 1792, an unsuccessful
satiric poem called "The Conspiracy of Kings" in which he attacked English conservatives and again, although in stronger
terms, warned the European monarchies that their downfall
was near. The poem produced less of a reaction than did *Advice
to the Privileged Orders*; however, the prediction was to come
true even sooner than Barlow had thought. In March, 1792,
King Leopold of Austria died, and Gustavus III of Sweden was
assassinated. Louis XVI had only a vestige of his position left;
and France declared war on Austria, the country that had most
vigorously supported Louis' monarchy.

At this moment Barlow again found himself in the middle of
international events. Shortly before the war began, Barlow departed for France on a mission, the purpose of which has never
been determined; but its intent was to be of some aid to France.
Ten weeks in France solidified his conviction that its revolution
was the salvation of Europe, and he returned to England and to
Ruth determined to proclaim his conviction. Barlow now kept a
watchful eye on the progress of the French government. The
army was preparing to export liberty to all of Europe, and, by
the fall of 1792, it was clear that France was about to establish
a republican government. Once again Barlow felt himself called
upon to give advice, this time in the form of *A Letter to the
National Convention*, which he had Thomas Paine deliver to the
convention in October, 1792. In the letter, which was enthusi-
astically written and cordially received, Barlow urged that the
people be allowed to govern themselves; and he set down very

specific principles for the French government to follow, including many of the principles already in use in the United States. The details of the document are discussed in a later chapter.

Barlow was well known, of course, to many members of the convention; his earlier *Advice to the Privileged Orders* had been read and discussed by most of these men; but *A Letter to the National Convention* fixed his reputation among the French leaders, who rewarded him by making him an honorary citizen of France, an award owned by Barlow's friend, Thomas Paine, and also by Alexander Hamilton, James Madison, and George Washington. Once more, full of revolutionary zeal and with the English government about to try him for sedition, Barlow left for Paris, again without Ruth, to deliver a letter of congratulations from the Constitution Society to the convention, a letter which he read on November 24, 1792. The response by the delegates was overwhelming; Barlow was at last a man of prestige and fame in France.

At no time in its brief history did the French Revolution appear more certain of success than at the close of 1792, but it was not long before it began its rapid decline to the Reign of Terror. Barlow, who was a witness to this decline, risked his life to oppose its final stages. January, 1793, saw the execution of Louis XVI; and February witnessed the French declaration of war on England, turning many English and American liberals against France and causing Barlow's name to be vilified in England—much to Ruth's fear and embarrassment.

Barlow, however, retained his optimism; he was electioneering. At the urging of some of the leaders of the French government, Barlow decided to enter the election for delegate to the National Convention from Savoy, located in the southeast corner of France. Although Barlow did not give himself much chance of victory, he was vitally interested in the new constitution that the convention was to prepare. While campaigning during the last part of 1792 and the beginning of 1793, Barlow became involved in a proposal to annex peacefully the Italian province of Piedmont which lay next to Savoy in the Alps. Pamphleteer that he was, Barlow decided to write another letter, this time to the people of the province to be annexed; and in this way he hoped to prepare them to welcome French republicanism when it came in the spring. In *A Letter to the People of Piedmont*, he argued that the French Revolution was of great benefit to the French people and would be equally beneficial to the people of Piedmont. Understandably, the letter was suppressed in Piedmont; and, after his election defeat, Barlow gave little additional thought to the people of Piedmont, although he did have the letter printed in English with *The Political Writings of Joel Barlow* in 1796.

The hills and valleys of Savoy looked very much like New England to a lonely Joel Barlow. He had not seen his home for nearly five years nor Ruth for several months. His thoughts of America and his friends were given visual significance when he was unexpectedly served a common New England dish of cornmeal mush—"hasty pudding." This culinary reunion caused Joel to write a mock-epic extolling the virtues of the dish. Beginning with the growing of the corn and culminating with the proper way to eat it, the poem traces, making use of elaborate epic machinery and properly inflated diction, the entire process of changing corn into pudding. An engaging performance, it is as entertaining today as it was to its first readers. Barlow, who thought it a trivial piece, did not bother to print it until 1796; but it remains today Barlow's best poem and his most anthologized composition. Barlow's biographer says that it "is worth a dozen *Visions of Columbus* or *Columbiads*,"[24] and he is probably right. But it is no small irony that the man who wanted to be known most of all as the epic poet of America is best known today for his poem about corn-meal mush.

After much lonely waiting, Barlow finally convinced Ruth that it was safe for her to travel to Paris; and in June, 1793, they were reunited—just in time to witness the horrors of the Reign of Terror. By the winter of that year, many of Barlow's friends and former allies were guillotined when the more extreme party headed by Robespierre gained control. Perhaps only Barlow's position as an American citizen prevented him from being one of the thousands executed during these hysterical months. Even Barlow's friend, Thomas Paine, spent almost a year in prison, being released only after the direct intervention of James Monroe, the new American minister.

With the collapse of constitutional government in France, Barlow had time to look into other affairs. Despite the Reign of Terror, he was convinced that France would return to republican principles when the surrounding countries realized that she could not be defeated. Barlow, therefore, decided that the best way he could help France was to keep her economically sound by seeing that she was supplied with necessary goods. As a citizen of a neutral country, he was able to do so—and increase the size of his own bank account as well.

Barlow reentered business with considerably more experience than he had brought to the earlier and disastrous Scioto affair. He was now a poet and politician of renown, a master of European intrigue, a citizen of both France and America, and an internationalist acquainted with many of the leading figures in Europe, and he was also fluent in French. In short, he was in an ideal position to act as a middleman for goods going into and out of France; and, if the activity was not quite legal, he could always excuse it as a patriotic service to his second country.

In order to expedite his business ventures, Joel and Ruth left for Hamburg, Germany, in the spring of 1794, hoping to use this international port as a base for their operations. Business flourished as thousands of ships flocked to the port to unload supplies to be shipped into France. Barlow acted as a middleman for a sizable portion of these goods; and, when he left Germany in late summer, 1795, he did so a wealthy man. Barlow had finally amassed the fortune that would free him to spend as much time as he wished on his poetry, one of the primary reasons he had left America to seek his fortune in the first place. But, at a time when he could have returned triumphantly, other, even more perilous adventures awaited Joel Barlow—adventures that postponed his return to poetry for nearly two years.

When Barlow arrived in Paris, he met for the first time a man who was to be his lifelong friend, the new American minister to France, James Monroe; and he renewed many old friendships, including one of the Connecticut Wits, David Humphreys. Humphreys was in Europe as minister to Portugal, and he was in Paris to find a man to handle the delicate negotiations with the pirates of Barbary. For centuries the ruling Turks of Algiers, Tripoli, and Tunis capriciously declared war on those countries

which sailed ships in the Mediterranean. During these periods of war, they seized shipping, divided the plunder among themselves, and kept the sailors for ransom. After a profitable period of plunder had passed, they then agreed to a peaceful settlement at great profit to themselves and released the prisoners. Then, at the first flimsy excuse, war was again declared, and the cycle began once more.

The United States at this point was attempting to negotiate a treaty with the regency of Algiers that would open the shipping lanes and release American prisoners, who were being subjected to all the indignities and cruelties of slaves. Since the ruling Dey was unpredictable and without conscience, a negotiator of great firmness and tact was needed; and, after some thought, Barlow accepted the position urged on him by his old friend, Humphreys, and by his new friend, Monroe. Early in 1796, Barlow sailed for Algiers, carrying with him 162,530 livres worth of jewels with which he hoped to gain the favors of the Dey. For the next twenty-one months Barlow's life was filled with dangerous international intrigue and constant frustration, for more than once his life depended on the whim of the Dey.

Briefly, Barlow's role in these affairs was as follows: Six months before his arrival in Algiers, a treaty had been signed between the regency and the United States. The United States received freedom of the seas, the right to use Algerine ports, and the release of prisoners held in Algiers. In return, Algiers received nearly one million dollars. Barlow's job was to keep the treaty open until the money came, which could and did take many months. That Barlow accomplished this task is incredible and a tribute to his diplomacy. Knowing that the treaty at best would be only temporary, Barlow used every device possible to placate the impatient Dey. He obtained the prisoners' release by paying the Dey money Barlow had just borrowed from him, and he even obtained a favorable treaty with Tunis by playing on the Dey's pride and vanity. At one point, the Dey was prepared to destroy his rival and compatriot of the Barbary shore if it did not accede to Barlow's demands.

Finally in June, 1797, Barlow sailed for Marseilles; and, after forty days of fumigation for the plague, he was reunited with Ruth. Barlow's experiences in Algiers strengthened his humani-

tarian impulses and also his resolve to domesticate himself and to spend his remaining years by the side of Ruth—a resolution he failed to keep. In a letter to Ruth he said, "I do not value the commission of any Government so much as to do good to humanity."[25] And, during the first few months following his return to Paris, Barlow successfully avoided politics. He enjoyed life in Paris and began planning a history of the French revolution, which he never wrote. The Barlows even talked of returning to America as soon as the weather was favorable in 1798. Once again, however, Barlow found himself forced into a position where political entanglement was unavoidable. Relations between France and the United States were deteriorating rapidly. Napoleon was solidifying his hold on the French government, and the Directory had ordered the French navy to capture American ships bound to or from British ports and to confiscate the cargo. The popular minister to France, James Monroe, had been recalled; sent to replace him was a pro-British, anti-French Federalist, Charles Pinckney, whom the French refused to receive. Efforts at negotiating a treaty between France and the United States ended in a crisis when the XYZ affair was made known in America. John Adams, who had narrowly defeated Jefferson for the presidency in 1796, was a Federalist; and, although Adams remained rational throughout the crisis, his party leaders were clamoring for all-out war against France. The two countries seemed to be sliding inevitably toward total war, and America began to arm.

Barlow felt himself compelled to do all he could to avoid conflict, and the result was a series of letters to America in which he urged the president to reopen negotiations with France; attacked, often bitterly, the Federalists who urged war; and presented, in mature and reasoned prose, his own idea concerning national government. In a letter to his brother-in-law, Senator Abraham Baldwin, a copy of which also went to Vice-President Jefferson, Barlow expressed dismay and anger that the United States under Federalist John Adams made no effort to reestablish friendly relations with France; in fact, he felt that the Federalists were intentionally trying to force a crisis. Unfortunately for Barlow, the letter was stolen and printed by a rabble-rousing Republican from Vermont, Senator Matthew

Lyon, who used it as an excuse to test the Alien and Sedition Acts just passed by Congress.

The published letter served to make complete Barlow's break with his old friends, the Connecticut Wits, and with many of his old Yale classmates. He was regarded as a traitor and as an atheist. Noah Webster, always a champion of American purity and the foe of European degeneracy, succinctly gave his view of the cause for this change in Joel: "The contemptuous manner in which you speak of the President and the Senate of America is striking proof of the effect of atheism and licentious examples on the civility and good manners of a well-bred man. You went from America with a good character . . . in divesting yourself of religion, you have lost your good manners."[26]

But Barlow was not finished writing letters. In November, 1798, he sent a letter to George Washington, the newly re-called commander-in-chief, urging him to use all his influence to bring about negotiations with the French; and in 1799, Barlow published *Letters from Paris*, directed to the citizens of the United States. In the first, published on March 4, he attempted to explain his position concerning his letter to Baldwin, which was published without his permission; in the second, published December 20, he warned the United States against losing the foundation of its superior type of government, "representative democracy, and the federalization of the states." By the end of the century, Barlow's reputation in America had reached its lowest point; but, ironically, with the election of Jefferson in 1800, his basic position was vindicated.

The change that had taken place in Barlow during the last twelve years was indeed significant. He was experienced and pro-ficient in a number of different fields, including politics, com-merce, and diplomacy. He had lived through some of the most interesting and dangerous experiences of those years. And he had sloughed off the conservatism in politics and religion that he had brought with him from Connecticut. The change is de-scribed, in satiric form, by Richard Alsop in the *Hartford Courant* during the height of the Federalist attack:

> His wandering wits, and cunning call'd in,
> Writes o're "*his book*" to Parson Baldwin. . . .
> What eye can trace this Wisdom's son,—

> This "jack-at-all-trades, good *at none*,"
> This ever-changing, Proteus mind,—
> In all his turns, thro' every wind;
> From telling sinners where to go to,
> To speculations in Scioto, . . .
> From morals pure, and manners plain,
> To herding with Monroe and Paine,
> From feeding on his country's bread,
> To aping X, and Y, and Z [ed],
> From preaching Christ, to Age of Reason,
> From writing psalms, to writing treason.[27]

As this poem indicates, Barlow's native country turned her back on him, and his adopted country betrayed the trust he had in her; but his muse was always faithful. During the years between 1800 and Barlow's return to America in 1804, he resumed work on several projects, including the scientific poem, "The Canal: A Poem on the Application of Physical Science to Political Economy in Four Books," and the complete revision of *The Vision of Columbus.*

While Barlow was embroiled in transatlantic politics, he and Ruth took a young man into their household by the name of Robert Fulton, an ex-painter from Pennsylvania with plans for intercity systems of canals and, eventually, even bigger plans for a submarine and a steamboat, both of which were financed in part by Joel Barlow. In the Yale Library is the manuscript of the beginning of a poem never completed called "The Canal." The poem was to be a joint effort with Barlow supplying the poetry and Fulton the technical details. Both Barlow and Fulton regarded the canal as an instrument of greater democracy because it would bring the people more closely together and would strengthen the economy of the country. In addition, they saw the canal as a symbol of American democracy united with "young Science." In a selection labeled simply "A Passage," Barlow explains why the Western world had progressed so swiftly:

> The March of Man! how slow his dull career
> In Eastern Climes! how swift and splendid here!
> Tis Freedom's force that works the wondrous odds
> Freedom the friend of man, the bane of kings and gods.

Democracy and rationality—in 1800 these were two pillars of Barlow's philosophy. His nonliterary concerns during these years reflected these beliefs just as completely as his revisions of *The Vision of Columbus* did.

Experiments with Fulton's submarine and steamboat and Ruth's lengthy illness forced the Barlows several times to postpone plans for a return to America. Ever since Thomas Jefferson had become president, the Barlows were eager to depart—a desire strengthened by Joel's increasing disillusionment with affairs in France. Jefferson, meanwhile, had a very specific reason for wishing Barlow's return to America: the Federalists were busy writing a history of the young republic which would present, Jefferson rightly believed, a biased interpretation of history. Jefferson therefore wanted his side represented, and he offered every assistance to Barlow if he would agree to write the history. It was, of course, a rare opportunity, but one, unfortunately, that Barlow never accepted completely. The Barlow Collection at Yale contains "Notes for history of U.S.—between 1801–1810," notes and fragments left by Barlow at the time of his death. It reveals a pro-Republican view of history and also reveals Barlow's sense of mission in passages such as this: "My predecessor the *Federalist* of 1788 showed the importance of *adopting* the Constitution; my object is to show the importance of *preserving* it." Unfortunately, the history was never finished; Barlow had other interests to occupy his time.

IV   *Return and Revision*

In August, 1804, after fifty-two days of continuous seasickness, Joel and Ruth Barlow at last arrived in the United States. For Joel, seventeen years had passed since he had left America as a naïve young man, and fifteen years had passed since Ruth had left her country in search of her husband. But America had also changed. Jefferson, who was completing his first term of office, was demonstrating to the world the validity of the republican principles which Barlow had championed. The struggling young country that Barlow had left in 1788 was now a prosperous nation; it had doubled in size; it was unlimited in promise; and it enjoyed a sizable portion of international trade. No longer was it an experiment; it was now an example, and Barlow justifiably took some pride both in his country and in his small role in shaping it. Now Barlow hoped to retire to an active life of leisure in Washington and to work on several projects which he felt would contribute still more to America's development: a completion of his history; the publication of his revised *Vision*; and, a special project, the establishment of a national university in Washington which would be "an institution of much more extensive and various utility than anything of the kind that has hitherto existed."[28]

But, first of all, the Barlows had to have a home. Although they still had friends and relatives in Connecticut, whom they visited shortly after returning from Europe, Barlow decided to settle in Washington in order to be close to the many public officials he had met during his residence abroad, not the least of whom was the president. On November 29, 1804, the Barlows rented several rooms in a Washington boardinghouse; and, following the publication of *The Columbiad* in 1807, he and Ruth decided to purchase an old mansion between Georgetown and Washington on the banks of Rock Creek. It offered a splendid view of the Potomac and the Capitol, and it was to be a cultural and political center of Washington life during the administrations of two presidents. Because the building's original name, "Belair" was in frequent use, Barlow changed it to "Calorama," a Greek word meaning "fine view," and later to "Kalorama."

Barlow's literary and social activities during this time were many. In 1806 a pamphlet appeared in Washington which described a plan for a school which was several generations ahead of its time in America but which Barlow hoped would be legislated into being before long. *Prospectus of a National Institution, to be Established in the United States* described something that comes close to being the modern university; and it was to "combine the two great objects, *research* and *instruction*." Barlow saw the school as a place where learned men could gather, pooling their knowledge and utilizing common resources, as well as a place where the youth could be instructed in most branches of theoretical and technical knowledge. Barlow's bill never left committee, however, partly because the Federalists feared a Republican scheme to establish a source of continuous power and partly because it simply cost too much. Both Barlow and Jefferson, of course, placed much of their hope for a democratic America on the education of the young and on the free dissemination of knowledge. An intelligent and well-informed electorate would insure the success of the American form of government. Barlow proposed his institution for the same reason that he had toiled in France and Algiers, had suffered personal attacks, and had continued to work on his *Vision*—a belief that he could contribute to the growing glory of America.

Because Barlow saw his revision of *The Vision of Columbus* as a "patriotic legacy to my country,"[29] he made extensive revisions and additions to it right up to the time it went to press. Despite his New England frugality and his Republican principles, Joel decided to give the very best appearance to what he now frankly called his "Epic," and he gave it the more epic-sounding name of *The Columbiad*. In preparation for this climactic event in his life, he and Ruth moved to Philadelphia, the printing center of America, to oversee all the details. Meanwhile, in England, the ever present Fulton was having illustrations made befitting the importance of the poem. He himself drew the preliminary sketches and commissioned a member of the Royal Academy to paint the pictures. The poem was published with eleven engravings, plus Fulton's own painting of Barlow, which appeared as a frontispiece. The care that went into the printing of the book was matched by the care taken with the illustrations. A large eighteen-point type was used on the finest paper available; and the poem, in quarto size, was enclosed in a beautiful leather cover with gold stamping. The result was the finest book that America had ever produced; but, unfortunately, it was also one of its dullest pieces of literature. In trying to make an epic out of a more modest philosophical poem, Barlow allowed every pretension to shine through. Since the poem itself is discussed in a later chapter, it is enough to add here that it is one of the world's great failures.

With the establishment of Jefferson's republicanism, Barlow had hoped that his days of controversy were over; but such was not the case. Even with the epic, which was Barlow's gift to America, people began to choose sides. Fulton, of course, praised it unreservedly; Noah Webster liked most of the Americanisms and modified spellings which Barlow had included, although he objected strenuously to certain "atheistical" ideas contained in the poem.[30] Thomas Jefferson commented on the beauty of the binding, but he confessed that he had not found time to read the poem (and he probably never did). Barlow's old classmate, President Josiah Meigs of the University of Georgia, bestowed upon his friend an honorary doctor of laws degree.

The reviews ranged from absurd praise to embarrassing contempt. The *London Monthly Magazine* said that it transcended "anything which modern literature has to boast, except the Paradise Lost of Milton." The *Philadelphia Portfolio* attacked its "bathos" and "ludicrous alliteration," and the important English *Edinburgh Review* published a sixteen-page attack on American presumptuousness as well as on *The Columbiad*'s weaknesses, although admitting that, among American writers, Barlow was probably the best—a statement that does not necessarily imply praise.

After the publication of *The Columbiad*, Barlow spent less and less time with literature, for he believed that his great work was finished. Although he wrote a number of occasional pieces in prose and poetry, made slight revisions in *The Columbiad*, and continued to work sporadically on the history for Jefferson, he and Ruth planned to spend their remaining years at "Kalorama," on the periphery of government affairs and surrounded by friends. Between 1807 and 1811, Barlow served unofficially as adviser to both Jefferson and Madison, sustained a sizable correspondence with numerous friends, became involved in the social affairs of the capital, and, gradually, developed into a kind of elder statesman, whose opinions were sought, especially in regard to relationships with France.

These were happy years for the Barlows in spite of Ruth's continued ill-health and their lessening contact with their "son," Robert Fulton, who had proved the feasibility of his steamboat, in the spring of 1807. In a letter to Barlow shortly after the famous successful run to Albany, Fulton wrote: "I had a light breeze against me the whole way, both going and coming, and the voyage has been performed wholly by the power of steam. I overtook many sloops and schooners beating to windward and parted with them as if they had been at anchor. The power of propelling boats by steam is now fully proved. . . ."[31] The Barlows had hoped that Fulton would marry Clara, Ruth's sister, and live at "Kalorama"; instead, he married an Englishwoman, causing a temporary cooling of their friendship.

A brief glance at several of Barlow's literary productions demonstrates the occasional nature of his verse and prose during the last years of his life. Early in 1807, a testimonial dinner was held for Captain Merriwether Lewis, who had just returned from his exploration of the Louisiana Territory. The event and the achievement caused Barlow to burst forth with a poem commemorating the occasion, "Ode on Captain Lewis," which was read to the guests by a Mr. Beckley. The lines jogged along monotonously, making all sorts of exaggerated claims. One quatrain, in which he urged the changing of the river's name to Lewis, suffices:

> Then hear the loud voice of the nation proclaim;
>   And all ages resound the decree:
> Let our occident stream hear the young hero's name
>   Who taught him his path to the sea.

In prose, Barlow reached one of the high points of his literary career when he gave a July 4 oration in Washington. Even by 1807, July 4 speeches were almost always deadly combinations of empty bombast and chauvinistic fervor. No one expected Barlow's to be any different. The result, however, was a closely reasoned and reasonable argument for America's future greatness. No longer was he relying on some vague concept of inevitable progress or on naïve faith in the people. Fully aware of the direction of France's attempt at democracy, he now insisted upon the education of the masses so that they could intelligently govern themselves: "It is not intended that every citizen should be a judge or a general or a legislator. But every citizen is a voter; and if he has not the instruction necessary to enable him to discriminate between the characters of men, to withstand the intrigues of the wicked and to perceive what is right, he immediately becomes a tool for knaves to work with; he becomes both an object and an instrument of corruption; his right of voting becomes an injury to himself and a nuisance to society"

(Works, p. 11). Howard called the *Oration at Washington* "Barlow's smoothest, most highly polished prose work";[32] it is certainly one of the best things he ever wrote.

V   *The Final Journey*

The Barlows' happy life at "Kalorama" was soon to end. Once again, Joel had accepted a request to serve his country; and once again, Joel and Ruth would be separated; however, this time there would be no reunion. Napoleon, in 1811, was sweeping across Europe and was about to invade Russia. The time was right, so President Madison and his secretary of state, James Monroe, thought, for a closer agreement between France and the United States. Joel Barlow, although still a controversial figure, was the obvious choice for the task; and in August, 1811, he left for France, without hope for success in his mission and with little hope of ever returning. Barlow seems to have had a strange premonition of his death, even though he was healthy and only fifty-seven years old. Shortly after leaving, he wrote to Fulton, saying, "I have left my country, possibly and why not probably forever. . . . I go with an ardent wish, but without much hope of doing good,—and with the full intention, tho with a feeble hope of living to return."[33] And, earlier, after agreeing to go to France, he gave Fulton directions for publishing his collected works, choosing those works which he felt best reflected the contributions he had made to his country and his hopes for America. The list, now in the Harvard Library, follows:

The Works Should Be Printed in the
following order.

Vol. I

The Columbiad—with its notes to follow at the end of the volume.

Vol. II

1. Advice to the Privileged Orders.
2. Letter to the National Convention.
3. Letter to the people of Piedmont.
4. Two letters to the citizens of the United States & one
   to George Washington.

5. Prospectus of a National Institution.
6. Oration at Hartford.
7. Oration at Washington.
8. Gregoire's Letter on The Columbiad.
9. Barlow's reply.
10. Gregoire's Second Letter.
11. Letter on the life of Thomas Paine.
12. The Conspiracy of Kings.
13. Hasty-Pudding.
14. Elegy on Titus Hosmer.
15. Ode on Captain Lewis.

Arrived in France, Barlow pursued his mission for more than a year without much success. International diplomacy, even then, was incredibly complex; but Barlow's primary objective was quite clear: avert war with both England and France and open American shipping, now restricted by both these countries. Napoleon, about to begin his Russian campaign, needed America's neutrality; and he dangled before Barlow the possibility of success while having no intention of allowing American shipping free access to the Continent. The British also prohibited American shipping with a blockade of the entire coast. Even after the United States declared war on England on June 17, 1812, Napoleon made no attempt to complete a treaty between the United States and France, which Barlow was trying desperately to work out. By now, Napoleon, completely enmeshed in the Russian campaign, cared little about relations with the United States.

But, during the fall of 1812, the war began to go badly for the French, who suddenly decided that a treaty with the United States would be to their advantage. Barlow was invited to come to the lines in Lithuania to conclude the treaty. Depressed by the thought of a fourteen-hundred-mile journey through wintry, war-torn northern Europe, Barlow and his nephew, Tom Barlow, who served as his secretary, nevertheless said goodby to Ruth and left for the front. Twenty-three days later, the Barlow carriage arrived in Wilna, Lithuania, which was serving as Napoleon's headquarters.

Although Barlow wrote letters to his wife which were occasionally optimistic and often amusing, he was becoming aware of Napoleon's imminent defeat and of the absurdity of the entire campaign. During his two-week stay, he wrote a poem, "Advice to a Raven in Russia," which is unlike anything he had ever written. In 1793, Barlow, in a state of pleasant homesickness, had written a mock-epic about hasty pudding, his most engaging work. In 1812, in Europe once again, he composed a bitter attack against man's greed and inhumanity. In the poem, he explains to the raven that no matter how far it travels, it will find food provided by Napoleon's army. The poem ends with a powerful plea for Napoleon's total destruction:

> War after war his hungry soul requires,
> State after state shall sink beneath his fires,
> Yet other Spains in victim smoke shall rise
> And other Moskows suffocate the skies,
> Each land lie reeking with its peoples slain
> And not a stream run bloodless to the main.
> Till men resume their souls, and dare to shed
> Earth's total vengeance on the monster's head,
> Hurl from his blood-built throne this king of woes,
> Dash him to dust, and let the world repose.[34]

The circle was ironically complete. Joel Barlow, who, in his youth, saw the hope for mankind in the French Revolution, now violently damned the monster that had issued from it. The poet who above all preached faith in mankind ended his life cursing man's folly.

The horror and the death of Napoleon's retreat across Poland was observed by Barlow through the carriage window as he and Tom fled before the Russian armies. Joel caught cold riding continually in a subzero carriage; and, finally, on December 21, 1812, he died of pneumonia. Joel Barlow, who dedicated his life to his country, remains buried in an obscure grave in Poland.

CHAPTER 2

The Vision of Columbus

WITHIN ONE year after graduation from Yale, Joel Barlow had completed a detailed plan for his long poem, *The Vision of Columbus*; however, eight years passed before the poem found its way to the public. The Yale Library has a manuscript of this plan dated August, 1779; but either this plan or an earlier version had been completed by June when Timothy Dwight commented favorably on it.[1] This early plan clearly shows that Barlow knew even at this time what he hoped to accomplish with his poem. The following extract appears at the beginning of his book-by-book outline:

A Plan for a Poem on the subject of America at large designed to exhibit the importance of this country in every point of view, as the noblest and most elevated part of the earth, and reserved to be [the] last and greatest theatre for the improvement of mankind in every article in which they are capable of improvement. The Poem will be rather of the philosophic than the epic kind. The machinery is simple, and it is hoped will be natural. As an Angel is imployed [*sic*] in unfolding these scenes to Columbus, nothing ought to be mentioned but what is important to the happiness of mankind, of whom these superior beings are always considered as the guardians. The circumstances of Columbus after his last return from America are well known to be very melancholy. Queen Isabella, his only benefactress, is dead, the king refuses to fulfill the contract upon which the discoveries were undertaken. The unfortunate hero, after a life of toils and disappointments, for the good of mankind, is deserted by his friends, and insulted by his enemies. In this situation the Poem opens.[2]

Both the purpose of the poem, to extol the virtues of America, and the machinery, a vision in which an angel describes America's future to Columbus, are established in Barlow's mind at this early date.

Even more surprising is the close similarity between Barlow's plan for each book and the Arguments which precede each book of the final poem.[3] A look at the plan and Argument for Book One will demonstrate this. The Plan:

Book 1st
    Condition of Columbus. Night. Columbus's lamentation. Appearance
and speech of the Angel. His message to Columbus to repay his toils by
representing the importance of them. They ascend a mountain that looks
westward over the Atlantic. The continent of America draws into vision.
General appearance of America. Description of the Andes and other mountains thro the continent. Seas and coasts, rivers, lakes, forests, valleys, soil,
fruits, flowers, air, predominance of cold, animals.

The Argument:

Condition and soliloquy of Columbus. Appearance and speech of the Angel. They ascend the Mount of Vision, supposed to be on the western
coast of Spain. Continent of America draws into view, and is described by
the mountains, rivers, lakes, soil, temperature, and some of the natural
productions. (124)

Only two major changes were made in the final poem. A
reference at the end of Book Two to the story of Manco Capac,
the legendary founder of Peru, was expanded into a full book
and a half of examination of the legend and to this was added
a lengthy dissertation on his "genius and institutions" included
at the end of Book Two. The second important change was, as
might be expected, a considerable expansion of the material
about the Revolutionary War. A brief reference to "Independence" became another book-and-a-half treatment, beginning
with the invasion of the British army and ending with its defeat.
    Both the Plan and the Argument conclude with a vision of
the union of all nations that will bring peace, harmony, and
happiness to mankind. The Plan, however, contained a statement omitted from the poem: "Promotion of this happiness a
complete system of religion, as it is the end of all revelation and
the complete duty of man. Deism, superstition." Apparently,
the suspicion of revealed religion which became evident in Barlow's thinking during his stay in Europe was already beginning
to develop during the eight years between the Plan and the final
publication of his *Vision of Columbus.* One other idea expressed
in the original plan was dropped in the poem; the Plan contained
reference in Book Eight to "Female sex. Their importance in a
moral view. Misery occasioned to mankind for want of attention to them. The future progress in the advancement of science
and happiness." Barlow's early affinity for this subject might be

explained by the fact that he was then in the process of courting
Ruth. Although his love for Ruth did not diminish over the next
eight years, his thoughts concerning the female sex may have
become more objective.

I   The Vision of Columbus

Barlow hoped to accomplish two objectives in his Introduction to *The Vision of Columbus.* First, he realized that most
Americans knew little about the early years of their own country and other countries in the Western Hemisphere; therefore,
he decided to provide the necessary historical background so
that his reader could understand what had happened to Columbus and why. Barlow emphasized in his account of Columbus'
life the extreme frustration and hardship which he experienced
before, during, and after his voyages to the New World; and the
poet was careful to point out that Columbus had approached
both Italy, his native land, and Portugal, the country under
whose flag he had been sailing, before seeking aid from Spain;
and Columbus did so to eliminate possible charges of treason.
Barlow was also careful to indicate the kindness with which
Columbus treated the natives he found in the New World. Both
his successors, however, Francis de Bovadilla and Nicholas de
Ovando, destroyed his initial goodwill by their acts of cruelty.
Shortly before the defeat of Columbus and after the death of
his friend, Queen Isabella, Columbus was imprisoned;[4] and, during this imprisonment, the vision came to him "in order to satisfy his benevolent mind, by unfolding to him the importance of
his discoveries, in their extensive influence upon the interest
and happiness of mankind, in the progress of society."

The second objective of the Introduction was to justify Barlow's use of the vision framework instead of the more highly
regarded epic-narrative form, which he returned to in his *Columbiad.* The justification appears in the final paragraph of the
Introduction:

The author, at first, formed an idea of attempting a regular Epic Poem,
on the discovery of America. But on examining the nature of that event,
he found that the most brilliant subjects incident to such a plan would
arise from the consequences of the discovery, and must be represented in

vision. Indeed to have made it a patriotic Poem, by extending the subject to the settlement and revolutions of North America and their probable effect upon the future progress of society at large, would have protracted the vision to such a degree as to render it disproportionate to the rest of the work. To avoid an absurdity of this kind, which he supposed the critics would not pardon, he rejected the idea of a regular Epic form, and has confined his plan to the train of events which might be represented to the hero in vision. . . . (121)

In other words, Barlow simply took the vision section of what might have been his epic and made that the poem. Book One begins, therefore, with a view of Columbus in prison and near the end of his life. Lamenting his sorry state, he launches into a soliloquy in which he describes his first sight of the New World and his regret that he will see it no more:

> I traced new regions o'er the pathless main,
> Dared all dangers of the dreary wave.
> Hung o'er its clefts and topp'd the surging grave,
> Saw billowy seas, in swelling mountains roll,
> And bursting thunders rock the reddening pole,
> Death rear his front in every dreadful form,
> Gape from beneath and blacken in the storm;
> Till, tost far onward to the skirts of day,
> Where milder suns dispens'd a smiling ray,
> Through brighter skies my happier sails descry'd
> The golden banks that bound the western tide.
> And gave the admiring world that bounteous shore
> Their wealth to nations and to kings their power. (126)

In the midst of this depression, the Angel, unnamed in *The Vision*, comes to Columbus:

> Mild in the midst a radiant seraph shone,
> Robed in the vestments of the rising sun;
> Tall rose his stature, youth's primeval grace
> Moved o'er his limbs and wanton'd in his face,
> His closing wings, in golden plumage drest,
> With gentle sweep came folding o'er his breast,
> His locks in rolling ringlets glittering hung,
> And sounds melodious moved his heavenly tongue. (128)

As the Angel speaks, Columbus is released from bondage; and they ascend a mountain from where Columbus can view, as had Moses, the promised land. His voyage across the ocean is traced; and, in a series of swooping aerial views, the coasts of North and South America are described. Concentrating on the waterways, which would allow settlement to take place, Barlow catalogues the rivers from South America to Canada and then westward through the Great Lakes to the Mississippi River. In a part of his listing he describes the rivers of Virginia:

> He spoke; and silent tow'rd the northern sky,
> Wide o'er the realms the hero cast his eye;
> Saw the long floods pour forth their watery stores,
> And wind their currents to the opening shores;
> While midland seas and lonely lakes display
> Their glittering glories to the beams of day.
> Thy capes, Virginia, towering from the tide,
> Raised up their arms and branch'd their borders wide;
> Whose broad embrace in circling extent lay,
> Round the calm bosom of thy beauteous bay.
> Where commerce since has wing'd her channel'd flight
> Each spreading stream lay brightening to the light;
> York led his wave, imbank'd in mazy pride,
> And nobler James fell winding by his side;
> Back tow'rd the distant hills, through many a vale,
> Wild Rappahanock seem'd to lure the sail,
> While, far o'er all, in sea-like azure spread,
> The great Potowmac swept his lordly bed. (139–40)

After completing the geographical survey in Book One, Barlow turned in Book Two to an examination of the early inhabitants of America. Two questions come to Columbus' mind: Where did these people come from, and why are these inhabitants so different in appearance and in action? To the first of these questions the Angel replies that the Indians of South and Central America were descended from inhabitants of the Mediterranean area who were accidently swept out to sea, but that the Indians of North America came from Siberia. Since the civilizations of Mexico and Peru were far superior to anything found to the north of them, Barlow is able to imply the natural cultural superiority of Europe over Asia.

The second question asked by Columbus is more difficult for the Angel to answer and necessitates a pseudoscientific explanation. According to Barlow, man is comprised of the elements of the earth in varying proportions. As he moves from one climate and soil composition to another, the components of his body change gradually. To prove this concept, Barlow refers to the Dutch and English settlers who took on a slightly darker skin tone after coming to America. Furthermore, he said, the soul is affected by its physical environment, accounting for the violent behavior to which the savage is prone:

> The painted chiefs, in death's grim terrors drest,
> Rise fierce to war, and beat the savage breast;
> Dark round their steps collecting warriors pour,
> And dire revenge begins the hideous roar:
> While to the realms around the signal flies,
> And tribes on tribes, in dread disorder, rise,
> Track the mute foe and scour the distant wood,
> Wide as a storm, and dreadful as a flood;
> Now deep in groves the silent ambush lay,
> Or wing the flight or sweep the prize away,
> Unconscious babes and reverend sires devour,
> Drink the warm blood and paint their cheeks with gore. (149–50)

Temporarily at least, Barlow was in a difficult position. If his theory of environment were true, the European settlers should have been reduced to a band of savages within several generations. This conclusion, however, is avoided by a deft piece of illogic. The coming of a superior culture tends to reverse the process for an inferior one; therefore, the savages will gain "a fairer tint and more majestic grace" as they become civilized.

Observing the primitive mode of life of these people, Columbus asks if civilization and culture had ever flourished here. The Angel replies that Mexico under Montezuma had developed a stable and happy society; but, unfortunately, Cortez would destroy it:

> Now see, from yon fair isle, his murdering band
> Stream o'er the wave and mount the fated strand;
> On the wild shore behold his fortress rise,
> The fleet in flames ascends the darken'd skies.
> The march begins; the nations, from afar,
> Quake in his sight, and wage the fruitless war;
> O'er the rich provinces he bends his way,
> Kings in his chain, and kingdoms for his prey;
> While, robed in peace, great Montezuma stands,
> And crowns and treasures sparkle in his hands,
> Proffers the empire, yields the sceptred sway,
> Bids vassal'd millions tremble and obey;

> And plies the victor, with incessant prayer,
> Thro' ravaged realms the harmless race to spare.
> But prayers and tears and sceptres plead in vain,
> Nor threats can move him, nor a word restrain;
> While blest religion's prostituted name,
> And monkish fury guides the sacred flame:
> O'er fanes and altars, fires unhallow'd bend,
> Climb o'er the walls and up the towers ascend,
> Pour, round the lowering skies, the smoky flood,
> And whelm the fields, and quench their rage in blood. (162)

Columbus, saddened by this spectacle, expresses sorrow that he discovered America since his discovery had helped to produce such wanton destruction. The Angel, however, turns his attention to South America; and, in the remainder of Book Two and in all of Book Three, the Angel tells the story of Capac and Oella and of the founding of Peru.

Manco Capac and his wife, Oella, lived on a small island in Lake Titicaca. One day, while wandering near the future site of the city of Cuzco, young Capac came upon a band of warlike and primitive natives who had no concept of property or of governmental organization. Capac returned to his young wife and convinced her that they should go to these people and care for them as benevolent rulers. Oella, by tradition, had invented the spinning of yarn from cotton; and their garments permitted them to approach the natives robed in white, which the natives took as a sign of their divinity. Book Two ends with this discovery by the natives:

> The astonish'd tribes behold with glad surprize,
> The gods descended from the favouring skies:
> Adore their persons, robed in whining white,
> Receive their laws and leave each horrid rite;
> Build with assisting toil, the golden throne,
> And hail and bless the sceptre of the Sun. (175)

Book Three, which continues the story of Manco Capac, relates some of his adventures as Peruvian emperor. In a footnote in Book Two, Barlow said of the incident described in the following book: "I have thrown the episode into an epic form, and given it so considerable a place in the Poem, for the purpose of exhibiting *in action* the characters, manners and sentiments of the different tribes of savages, that inhabit the mountains of South-America" (167). The episode that Barlow refers to took place twenty-four years after Capac had assumed power. The Peruvians were attacked by a band of savages, whom they finally repelled. While giving an account of a peace journey which Capac's oldest son, Rocha, made, Barlow is able to describe several other tribes that Rocha met. First, he met a tribe of volcano worshipers who were offering human sacrifices and who worshiped storms; and, although his missionary work was less successful with them, he was allowed to pass through unharmed. Finally, he and his men reached the savage tribe with whom his people were at war. Zamor, their chief, ordered the immediate deaths of all except Rocha, who would be sacrificed later before the eyes of his mother.

Once again, the savages attacked the Peruvians, this time at dawn. At the moment of battle, however, an eclipse of the sun occurred, which Oella immediately took as a sign that something had happened to her son. As the sun reappeared, a warrior spotted Rocha about to be sacrificed on an altar; and the Peruvians who countercharged in fury were led by Manco Capac, who was determined to rescue his son unharmed and who was determined to kill Zamor. This intent he did in epic fashion and with heroic sweep:

> Like the black billows of the lifted main,
> Rolls into sight the long Peruvian train;
> A white sail, bounding, on the billows toot,
> Is Capac, striding o'er the furious host.
> Now meet the dreadful chiefs, with eyes on fire;
> Beneath their blows the parting ranks retire:
> In whirlwind-sweep, their meeting axes bound,
> Wheel, crash in air, and plough the trembling ground;
> Their sinewy limbs, in fierce contortions, bend,
> And mutual strokes, with equal force, descend;
> The king sways backward from the struggling foe,
> Collects new strength, and with a circling blow
> Rush'd furious on; his flinty edge, on high,
> Met Zamor's helve, and glancing, cleft his thigh.
> The savage fell; when, thro' the tyger-train,
> The driving Inca swept a widening lane;
> Whole ranks fall staggering, where he lifts his arm,
> Or roll before him, like a billowy storm;

Behind his steps collecting legions close,
While, centred in a circling ridge of foes,
He drives his furious way; the prince unties,   ,
And thus his voice—Dread Sovereign of the skies,
Accept my living son, again bestow'd,
To grace with rites the temple of his God.
Move, warriors, move, complete the work begun,
Crush the grim race, avenge the injured Sun. (223–24)

By the end of Book Three, the savages have been completely defeated; and Capac, in the tradition of the benevolent ruler, has offered them mercy.

Barlow told in verse the adventures of Manco Capac, adventures that illustrated the type of man and ruler he was. A detailed examination of the Peruvian government and Capac's lawmaking abilities, however, would have interrupted the flow of action, so Barlow decided to present this information in prose form at the end of Book Two in the first edition and at the end of the poem in later revised editions. With this essay, "A Dissertation on the Genius and Institutions of Manco Capac," Barlow took no chances that his readers might miss the point.

Barlow believed that the government set up by Manco Capac surpassed in effectiveness any government established in a barbaric or semicivilized land. He compared Capac to other rulers of barbarous people such as Moses, Lycurgus, Mahomet, and Peter of Russia; and he found that Capac equalled or surpassed the best qualities of each. A legislator of uncivilized tribes, he wrote, must tend to three items. First, he must be able to rule a great many people under one government. Second, he must make use of those principles consistent with human nature; and they must be universal and permanent to ensure the durability of the government. Third, he must make use of new knowledge and developments consistent with the principles of the government.

Capac's genius was exhibited in his ability to establish a stable government, to invest that government with religious authority, and to direct both the government and religion toward benevolent and humane action. Capac's political and social systems strongly resemble a blending of a benevolent monarchy and a feudal society. The king had absolute power and so much wealth that, according to Barlow, he was incorruptible. Beneath him were the nobles, the peasantry, and the servants; land was distributed by the king depending upon the size of the family so, again according to Barlow, the people were perfectly content with their positions in life. The king was also divine, thereby strengthening his position among the people and increasing the stability of his country.

These views seem strange when one considers Barlow's later democratic and Deistic positions, but some suggestions of later ideas do exist. First, Barlow emphasized that Capac came to his ideas by sheer reason rather than by divine or mystical insight; he could not possibly imitate earlier law givers because their examples were not available to him. Second, he admired the effective use to which Capac put religion rather than the inherent truth of it. Third, he went to great lengths to point out that Capac's religion was a benevolent one, worshiping the sun rather than the volcano or storms as other surrounding tribes did. And, fourth, in a later revision of his poem, Barlow modified his position by saying that investing a government with religious authority was the most effective type of government until the recent institution of representative republics, a type of government which came after most of *The Vision of Columbus* had been written.

Book Four continues the account of the Southern Hemisphere with a description by the Angel of the subsequent destruction of Peru by Pizarro and the murder of "unarm'd thousands" by Father Vincent Valverde, a priest who accompanied Pizarro and who gave church sanction to the slaughter. Columbus, despondent, replies:

> Why should I live to view the impending doom?
> If such dread scenes the scheme of heaven compose,
> And virtuous toils induce redoubled woes,
> Unfold no more; but grant a kind release,
> Give me, 'tis all I ask, to rest in peace. (230)

But the Angel assures Columbus that much good also resulted from his discovery of America.

First, the Seraph gives an account of the Reformation, an especially vital event in the light of Barlow's placing much blame for the devastation of Peru on a Catholic country and particularly on a priest of that country. In a series of time-spanning visions, the Angel describes Erasmus who began to question church authority; Martin Luther, "Fair light of heav'n, and child of deathless fame"; "fierce Loyola"; and, finally, the Spanish Inquisition which saw "Millions of martyr'd heroes mount the pyre."

Barlow then jumps to a description of Raleigh's landing in Virginia; and, after a brief account of the formation of the North American coast by the Gulf Stream, he proceeds, through the words of the Angel, to envision the peopling of North America, much to the delight of Columbus. These settlers, he said, will throw off the monarchies and superstitions of Europe, settle this land which offers unlimited possibilities without the temptation of instant wealth, and develop a state more ideal than any the world has known:

> A new creation waits the western shore,
> And reason triumphs o'er the pride of power.
> As the glad coast, by Heaven's supreme command,
> Won from the wave, presents a new-form'd land;
> Yields richer fruits and spreads a kinder soil,
> And pays with greater stores the hand of toil;
> So, call'd from slavish climes, a bolder race,
> With statelier step, these fair abodes shall trace;
> Their freeborn souls, with genius unconfined,
> Nor sloth can poison, nor a tyrant bind;
> With self-wrought fame and worth internal blest,
> No venal star shall brighten on the breast;
> No king-created name or courtly art
> Damp the bold thought, or sway the changing heart.
> Above all fraud, beyond the titles great,
> Heaven in their soul and sceptres at their feet,
> The sires of unborn nations move sublime,
> Look empires thro' and pierce the veil of time,
> The fair foundations form, and lead afar
> The palm of peace or scourge of barbarous war.
> Their following sons the godlike toil behold,
> In freedom's cause, unconquerably bold,
> Complete the toils, display their glories round,
> Domestic states and distant empires bound,
> Brave the dread powers, that eastern monarchs boast,
> Explore all climes, enlighten every coast;
> Till arts and laws, in one great system bind,
> By leagues of peace, the labours of mankind. (245–46)

The book ends with a short catalogue of the early settlers of America, including those who fled Archbishop Laud's church restrictions in the 1630's, Lord Baltimore and his followers, "heav'n-taught Penn," and various others who "Point their glad streamers to the western world."

Columbus and the Angel, sailing sublimely above the Western Hemisphere with two continents spread out conveniently beneath them, now begin to narrow their range in Book Five and to focus more sharply on the eastern half of the North American continent. After an opening description of some of the bloody conflicts between the settlers and the Indians, Barlow moves to an account of the French and Indian War, which he saw as the beginning of the colonists' movement toward independence, and to a description of young Washington, the hero of that struggle. At this point, a problem of some delicacy confronted Barlow. France, later to become a crucial ally in the War for Independence, had opposed the colonists who supported the British. In particular, Barlow had to describe Washington's magnificent performance against a foe which, in the next book, was praised. To this challenge Barlow had little trouble responding. In the first place, he insisted that this war was simply a transplant from the Continent, brought over primarily by the British. Second, the intentions of the French, "rob'd in white," were at least at first honorable; and, third, by concentrating on the majestic figure of Washington, Barlow was able to shift attention away from the French.

Washington's presence, according to Barlow, dominated the scene. Into the chaos and discouragement of the English "chiefs confus'd" and "hemm'd on every side" comes a "blooming warrior," "undaunted o'er the field of blood." The first description of Washington reveals Barlow's quite conscious attempt at achieving epic proportions.

> Fair on firey steed, sublime he rose,
> Wedg'd the firm files and eyed the circling foes;
> Then waved his gleamy sword, that flash'd the day,
> And, thro' dread legions, hew'd the rapid way,
> His hosts roll forward, like an angry flood,
> Sweep ranks away and smear their paths in blood;
> The hovering foes pursue the strife afar,
> And shower their balls along the flying war;

> When the brave leader turns his sweeping force,
> Points the flight forward—speeds his backward course;
> The foes fly scattering where his arm is wheel'd,
> And his firm train treads safely o'er the field. (258)

With the coming of peace, a great cloud descends over the land to open again some years later on the First Continental Congress with brief descriptions of various colonial leaders, including John Randolph, Franklin, the Adamses, and "immortal Hosmer," Barlow's late friend who received a full ten-line elegy complete with Columbus' tears; but Jefferson was barely mentioned.

As with the French and Indian War, the early stages of the Revolution were filled with confusion and despair. Once again, however, order and hope were restored by Washington, "Matured with years, with nobler glory warm, / Fate in his eye, and vengeance on his arm." The last part of Book Five catalogues the colonial heroes and battles from Lexington and Concord to the surrender of General Burgoyne at Saratoga in October, 1777 —a crucial victory because it prompted the French to enter the war officially; and on this note Barlow opens Book Six.

Most of this book describes the key battles leading up to the defeat of Cornwallis by Washington's troops and the French navy. The first part of the book, however, discusses the character and motives of a friend to the downtrodden "Great Louis," to whom *The Vision of Columbus* was dedicated, as well as the effect the American struggle for independence was having among the oppressed peoples of Europe. In metaphoric terms, Barlow describes the glow generated by the colonial quest for freedom:

> Thus all the eastern world, in glad amaze,
> Gaze on the scene and brighten as they gaze;
> Wake to new life, assume a borrow'd name,
> Enlarge the lustre and partake the fame.
> So mounts of ice, that polar skies invade,
> Unheeded stand beneath the evening shade;
> Yet, when the morning lights their glaring throne,
> Give back the day and imitate the sun. (283–84)

At last, the war concluded, Barlow turns to more "philosophical" interests relating to America's destiny. The final three books of the poem examine America's progress in such peaceful pursuits as commerce and the fine arts (Book Seven), the reasons for this progress (Book Eight), and America's, as well as

mankind's future greatness (Book Nine). Book Seven reveals
Barlow's basic ideas through the material he chose to discuss
and the progressive order of this material. Beginning with a
brief hymn to "sacred peace," Barlow returns Columbus and the
Angel to the early periods of settlement and traces America's
progress which had culminated recently in independence and,
according to Barlow, in a flourish of culture. First, the development of commerce is described, one necessary before the arts
could appear. Following the establishment of a firm economic
base, educational centers are founded to provide a source for
the dissemination of culture with Harvard, Yale, Princeton,
Pennsylvania, and even "growing Dartmouth," the school Barlow had attended briefly before going on to Yale. Coupled with
education, a foundation for democracy emphasized throughout
Barlow's life was religion, discussed at some length in *The Vision
of Columbus* but eliminated almost entirely in *The Columbiad*—
a change that reflects, of course, Barlow's own change in attitude
between 1787 and 1807. Now, however, religion plays a vital
role; its function, together with education, is

> To lead whole nations in the walks of truth,
> Shed the bright beams of knowledge on the mind,
> For social compact harmonize mankind,
> To life, to happiness, to joys above, . . . (304–5)

The major purpose of the colleges of Barlow's day was to prepare ministers, so the connection between religion and education is quite obvious, especially to Barlow, who had recently
been an army chaplain. But American civilization also developed
in other ways. In science, Barlow cites Franklin's invention of
the lightning rod, David Rittenhouse's telescope, and Thomas
Godfrey's quadrant. In painting, Benjamin West, John Singleton
Copley, and John Trumbull are mentioned. And in poetry, Barlow describes the activities of several of his fellow Connecticut
Wits, a description that remained essentially the same in *The
Columbiad*. Of the satirist, John Trumbull, he writes:

> His skillful hand
> Hurls the keen darts of Satire thro' the land;
> Pride, knavery, dullness, feel his mortal stings,
> And listening virtue triumphs while he sings;

of Barlow's good friend, Timothy Dwight:

> Fired with the themes by seers seraphic sung,
> Heaven in his eye, and rapture on his tongue,
> His voice divine revives the promised land,
> The Heaven-taught Leader and the chosen band.

And of his benefactor in the army, David Humphreys:

> See Humphreys glorious from the field retire,
> Sheathe the glad sword and string the sounding lyre;
> That lyre which, erst, in hours of dark despair,
> Roused the sad realms to urge the unfinish'd war. (311–12)

Before presenting his final view of America's future greatness, Barlow, in Book Eight, suspends the vision temporarily in order to present his own modest and rather vague epistemology, one not unlike that proposed by the Scottish common-sense philosophers, in answer to Columbus' question: "Why did not Heaven, with one unclouded ray, / All human arts and reason's powers display?" (315). In response to this question, Barlow catalogues the development of civilization, showing that at certain times man relied almost exclusively on his passions and at other times on his reasoning powers, by which Barlow apparently means some kind of deductive system in which man never questions his basic premise. Both sources of knowledge ignore observation by the senses and the inductive process; hence, Barlow thinks that they ignore man and his condition in society. Excessive passion results in "raging zeal"; excessive rationality, in "sceptic scorn."

The way to truth is between these two extremes; the source of all truth is the "one great moral Sense," God; and man's duty is a simple one, "To love the neighbor and adore the God." What man has lacked so far and what the Angel promises Columbus that man will soon have is a concern for his fellow man, for it alone can temper the extremes of hot faith and cold rationality.

Barlow is now faced with a philosophical problem that confronted other eighteenth-century optimists. If man is capable of knowing this middle way, why has it been kept from him so long? If the ultimate end is good, how can all the evil that has occurred so far be explained? Barlow responds with the popularized Leibnitzian logic that Voltaire attacked so effectively in *Candide.* God has allowed man to stumble and err because man must come to these answers himself. All the murder, destruction, intolerance, and foolishness of the world are necessary so that man may proceed toward the truth. All is for the best, and this is the best of all possible worlds.

Book Eight is a philosophical preparation for the vision of a future society which Barlow presents in the poem's final book. Application of Book Eight's epistemology will result in a better world; "soaring Science" and "blest Religion" will show man the way to truth by revealing "the image of the Maker's mind." Barlow places his hope for the future on the increasing interaction among men brought about by commerce and learning. As man's mind and interests reach across provincial boundaries, so will his limited and limiting national concerns. The result, inevitably, will be a world united by common understanding.

> No more the noble patriotic mind,
> To narrow views and local laws confined,
> 'Gainst neighbouring lands directs the public rage,
> Plods for a realm or counsels for an age;
> But lifts a larger thought, and reaches far,
> Beyond the power, beyond the wish of war;
> For realms and ages forms the general aim;
> Makes patriot views and moral views the same;
> Sees with prophetic eye in peace combined,
> The strength and happiness of human-kind. (348–49)

Columbus asks the Angel for a view of this perfect world. Although refusing to give this view because it would blind Columbus (and perhaps overtax Barlow's poetic powers and imagination), the Angel does allow Columbus two visions. The first, more heard than seen, involves the gradual harmonizing of the various languages of the world, paralleling, of course, the harmonizing of the societies themselves. Despite his pleasure with this outcome, Columbus cannot help thinking of the Tower of Babel and wondering why God allowed this confusion of tongues to occur. In another ingenious variation on the eighteenth-century theme of optimism, the Angel explains that it is only because of man's many languages that he felt forced to wander the earth, discovering and civilizing it. Had the early inhabitants spoken the same language, they would have been content to remain together. Columbus' own exploits, therefore, are the direct result of the Tower of Babel. Once again, Barlow is successful in showing how good may derive from evil.

The Angel's second and final vision is of a universal governing body. The inevitable result of mankind's uniting in larger and larger social and political units is a final and total unison which ushers in the millennium. This united world is not simply a symbol for Barlow, nor is his vision of the perfection of man. In a note attached to the fifth edition of his poem, he states, "It has long been the opinion of the author, that such a state of peace and happiness as is foretold in scripture, and commonly called the millennial period, may be rationally expected to be introduced without a miracle."[5] The poem's final vision is, therefore, a fitting climax to an account of man's social and moral progress. First, the government building is described:

> On rocks of adamant the walls ascend,
> Tall columns heave, and Parian arches bend;
> High o'er the golden roofs, the rising spires,
> Far in the concave meet the solar fires;
> Four blazing fronts, with gates unfolding high,
> Look, with immortal splendor, round the sky;
> Hither the delegated sires ascend,
> And all the cares of every clime attend. (356)

Then the delegates arrive:

> Now the dread concourse, in the ample dome,
> Pour thro' the arches and their seats assume;
> Far as the extended eye can range around,
> Or the deep trumpet's solemn voice resound,
> Long rows of reverend sires, sublime, extend,
> And cares of worlds on every brow suspend. (357)

And *The Vision of Columbus* ends by emphasizing the eighteenth-century virtues of harmony, regularity, and completeness:

> Bid one great empire, with extensive sway,
> Spread with the sun and bound the walks of day,
> One centred system, one all-ruling soul,
> Live thro' the parts, and regulate the whole. (357)

II   *Background of* The Vision of Columbus

The intellectual climate of New England during the time that Barlow was composing his *Vision of Columbus* reflected a number of related and opposing ideas. Leon Howard, writing in *Transitions in American Literary History*, described three paths to truth open to writers of this period: "that of pious communion with the divine being, that of neoplatonic intuition, and that of a formally defined common sense."[6] Barlow seems to ignore Puritanism as a means of revealing the truth; however, both his *Vision of Columbus* and Puritanism look forward to a future life that will be better than the present, the major difference being, of course, that man's perfection will be achieved on earth. As pointed out in the first chapter, Barlow was aware of Lord Kames and the Scottish common-sense philosophers; he had access to James Beattie's *Essay on the Nature and Immutability of Truth* as well as Kames's *Elements of Criticism*; and he was undoubtedly affected by the more moderate path to truth offered by this method: avoidance of both extreme rationality and extreme sentimentality.[7] However, any influence from the common-sense philosophers seems to have been supportive rather than formative. The philosophical basis for *The Vision of Columbus* was probably Barlow's own optimistic faith in the future and his age's belief in man's inevitable progress toward perfection.[8]

B. T. Spencer, in his excellent *The Quest for Nationality*, describes the self-conscious attempts on the part of early American writers to establish an independent and native American literature, a movement which swept Joel Barlow along with it. Contrary to what one might expect, a long tradition of literary nationalism had been established by the outbreak of the Revolutionary War. This nationalism was manifested, however, much more openly in the thematic concerns of the colonials than in the form their statements took. The Revolution, of course, increased these nationalistic concerns of American writers; in fact, many writers, including Joel Barlow, felt that the Revolution could provide a heroic past for the American poet even before it was ended.[9] During and immediately after the Revolution, nationalism became so rampant that no writer could be heard unless he included strong and patriotic references to America's struggles and to the inevitable progress of American democracy.[10] For Barlow in his *Vision*, this progress was inevitable because God was, in a vague sort of way, looking to the details. A later Barlow would shift the emphasis from God to a benign mechanical universe and then finally to man himself; the inevitability of progress, however, was always there.

The historical sources Barlow chose for his *Vision* can be traced quite easily. Barlow knew Homer from Pope's translation; the *Aeneid* in Latin; and, of course, Milton's *Paradise Lost*. The device of having an angel take Columbus to a high mountain in order to show him America's future is a direct imitation of the Raphael-Adam episode in Milton's poem, and in *The Vision of Columbus* Barlow criticized the *Iliad* because it glorified war and violence; thus he wrote his poem, partly at least, to counteract this tendency in epics. Barlow also had a copy of Voltaire's *Essay on Epic Poetry*,[11] and he undoubtedly found support in it for his own desire for a looser definition of the epic: less adherence to strict Neoclassical rules and the substitution of contemporary figures in place of Classical ones.

Historically, Barlow relied very heavily on secondary sources for the earlier accounts of the Western Hemisphere; but for the later history of the country, he used primary sources and his own experience. In his Introduction to *The Vision of Columbus*, Barlow referred to William Robertson's *The History of America*, a three-volume work, as being the only work capable of explaining all the allusions in the poem; and he relied very heavily on this history written by a Scotsman who had never visited America. The three other works Barlow used extensively for his treatment of South America were Garcilaso de la Vega's *The Royal Commentaries of Peru*, which contained a good bit of information about Manco Capac; Juan Francisco Marmontel's *The Incas: or The Destruction of the Battle of Peru*; and Don Alonzo de Ecrilla's *Araucana*, not translated into English but discussed by Voltaire in his *Essay on Epic Poetry*.[12]

III   *Barlow's Dinosaur*

On Tuesday, September 18, 1787, George Washington sent a gift copy of *The Vision of Columbus* to a Mrs. Penn. Accompanying the gift was a letter which Washington directed to be written, and it reads in part: "Gen l Washington takes the liberty of offering his respectful compliments to Mrs. Penn—and the Vision of Columbus. —It is one of several copies for which he subscribed some years ago and received since he came to this city. —To the merit, or demerit of the performance, the General can say nothing—not having had time to read it."[13] General Washington's experience was probably a representative one. Barlow sold enough copies of the book for it to be termed a financial success; but, apparently, very few people actually read it all the way through, a statement which is much truer today. Barlow's biographer calls the poem "a dinosaur in the clay pits of literary history."[14]

When judged by the critical standards of his time, as he should be, Barlow was a competent poet. He was able to write reasonably smooth heroic couplets; he had an awareness of the diction and devices used by his predecessors; and he was able to tell a story, discuss an idea, or project a vision with relative clarity. His failure undoubtedly can be attributed to many sources, but most of these can be put into one of two categories. First, Barlow had only the most rudimentary and mechanical notion of what possibilities the heroic couplet held. He read Pope, but all he saw were the elements common to the couplet—never what distinguished one couplet from another. He saw the two-line unit, he saw the iambic rhythm, he saw the caesura, he saw the balanced phrase; but he never felt the subtleties with which Pope could individualize a line. He never felt Pope's careful and sensitive manipulation of sounds and rhythms. In short, Barlow was not a Pope.

Closely allied with this deficiency—and, partly at least, the result of it—is the fact that, as James Woodress has said, the poem simply does not live. Only in brief passages, and they are widely scattered, do Barlow's stylistic encumbrances permit spirit to breathe through the lines. Only briefly does he use words which describe life or death rather than conventionalized reactions to and descriptions of these subjects; as a result, most of the poem plods wearily along.

The extent of Barlow's success and his failure can be seen in a short passage from Book Five in which Indians attack the colonists and are then repulsed:

> Thro' cultured fields, the bloody myriads spread,
> Sack the lone village, strow the streets with dead;
> The flames aspire, the smoky volumes rise,
> And shrieks and shouts redouble round the skies;
> Fair babes and matrons in their domes expire,
> Or burst their passage thro' the folding fire;
> O'er woods and plains promiscuous rave along
> The yelling victors and the driven throng;

The streams ran purple; all the extended shore
Is wrapped in flames and trod with steps of gore.
Till numerous hosts, collecting from afar,
Exalt the standard and oppose the war,
Point their loud thunders on the shouting foe,
And brave the shafted terrors of the bow.
When, like a broken wave, the savage train
Lead back the flight and scatter o'er the plain,
Slay their weak captives, leave their shafts in haste,
Forget their spoils and scour the distant waste,
As, when the morning sun begins his way,
The shadows vanish where he gives the day;
So the dark tribes, from brighter regions hurl'd,
Sweep o'er the heights and lakes, far thro' the wilder'd world. (253–54)

Barlow was at his best when using narrative, and the slaughter by Indians is an inherently interesting subject; however, Barlow does manage to use enough conventionalized and generalized terminology so that the impression is distant and vague rather than immediate and precise. Words and phrases such as "cultured fields," "bloody myriads," "strow the streets," "flames aspire," "numerous hosts," "savage train," and "the wilder'd world" dilute the effect. One couplet does carry considerably more impact than the rest of the passage, although, once again, a discrepancy exists between the force of the scene itself and Barlow's account of it: "The streams ran purple; all the extended shore / Is wrapped in flames and trod with steps of gore." The images of blood, burning homes, and the gore-covered feet of the Indians are powerful, particularly the last; and Barlow uses words such as "flames" and "gore" to describe this scene; however, he also calls on standardized diction with "streams ran purple" and "extended shore" while diminishing the impact of the second line by coupling "flames" and "gore" with the more generalized words, "wrapped" and "trod."

An examination of Barlow's use of the heroic couplet in this passage also reveals his strength and weakness. He used, of course, the closed couplet favored by the popular eighteenth-century poets, and he attempted to provide variety primarily by manipulation of the caesura. Each couplet is a self-contained unit adding its bit to the total narrative. The couplet "The flames aspire, the smoky volumes rise, / And shrieks and shouts redouble round the skies" is representative. The caesura in the first line allows the poet to present two, syntactically balanced, details of the scene; the four-syllable phrase in the first part of the line suggests in its quickness the sudden motion of the fire; but the six-syllable phrase which concludes the line suggests, by contrast, the slower motion of the smoke. The confusion and terror of the scene moves swiftly through the second line with no definite caesura (although the natural pause between subject and predicate does exist) and with the help of alliteration.

Another example of Barlow's conscious but rather heavy-handed attempt to manipulate the line for specific effects is found in the final line of the section. The alexandrine, which provides a punctuation-mark finish to the scene, is produced by the simple and unnecessary addition of "and lakes" to the line. The extra foot, however, does support the sweeping motion of the retreat which the poet is describing.

Barlow is even less successful in his more philosophical passages; for he uses many more vague generalities, clichés, and stock expressions. His ideas are often difficult to grasp, not because they are profound or unorthodox, but because Barlow's verbal smokescreen is difficult to penetrate. His prose pamphlets, which discuss these same ideas, are much clearer and more direct. Apparently Barlow believed that all he had to do to produce poetry was to "poetize" prose.

One final point must be made when evaluating the successes and failures of *The Vision of Columbus.* James Woodress believes that Barlow never successfully combines the philosophical and epic elements in the poem,[15] which brings one back to a look at Barlow's early plans for his work. Columbus was the hero who, although lacking heroic proportions, could be the eyes through which America could see its past, present, and future; but the real epic hero, as has been observed, of Barlow's *Vision* is America itself. Instead of frankly accepting this fact, as Whitman did a century later, Barlow used the conventionalized epic tradition to describe Columbus or one of the other heroes, Washington for instance, while at the same time he was searching for and finding reasons that would explain America's unique accomplishments and opportunities. The poem never successfully blends these two parts into a unified whole.

CHAPTER 3

Vision and Revision

JOEL BARLOW'S uniqueness as a Connecticut Wit lies in the fact that he alone made the switch from Calvinistic Federalist to Deistic Jeffersonian, a switch that can be seen dramatically in the difference between *The Vision of Columbus* of 1787 and Barlow's extensive revision of that poem published twenty years later as *The Columbiad.* During most of those twenty years Barlow was in Europe where he became acquainted with the liberal religious and political thinkers of both England and France, as well as with such distinguished American visitors as James Monroe and Thomas Jefferson. The prose, mostly in pamphlet form, that was written during this period, especially in the 1790's, reflects ideas which Barlow later incorporated into his *Columbiad,* proof that these ideas were held by Barlow a number of years before his grand epic appeared.

I *The 1793 Edition*

Largely ignored by critics is a revised edition of *The Vision of Columbus* which Barlow had printed in Paris in 1793 at about the time he was most actively participating in international and particularly in French politics. Of this edition, Leon Howard, in his excellent study of the Connecticut Wits, said only that "While correcting it for publication in 1793 he must have become aware that the poem demanded drastic changes if it were to reflect his mature opinions,"[1] the implication being that this awareness was not put into action until 1807. James Woodress, Barlow's biographer, has ignored this edition completely. Actually, despite Barlow's modest subtitle "the Fifth Edition, Corrected" and his comment in the "author's advertisement" that he had added "some few additional notes which he has found leisure to make," Howard's assumptions are borne out not only in the later *Columbiad* but also in this revised edition; for Barlow more than simply corrected errors and added notes: he also changed, deleted, or added passages that reflect major shifts in his religious and political thinking, and he reveals attempts on his part to improve the esthetic quality of the poem.

Most of Barlow's attempts to improve the quality of the poetry involve deletions of generalized descriptions and the substitution of more detailed description as well as omission of summary and transitional material. For instance, in Book One of the first edition, a description of the Mississippi River concludes with this general statement: "There lies the path some future ship shall trace, / And waft to these wide vales thy kindred race" (143). In the fifth edition, this couplet is changed slightly and preceded by a more detailed account of the course of the waters:

> To his broad bed their tributary stores,
> Arkansa here, and there Missouri pours,
> Rouge, from the western wild, his channel fills,
> Ohio, gather'd from a thousand hills,
> The Black, the Yazoes fed by Georgian springs,
> And Illinois his northern tribute brings,—
> There lies the path thy future sons shall trace,
> And spread o'er these wide realms the glory of thy race. (I, 487–94)[2]

And several pages later, Barlow omitted the final fourteen lines of Book One which summarized the movement of the poem to that point:

> When now the chief had travel'd with his eyes,
> O'er each fair clime that meets the incumbent sky;
> The stream, the mountain, forest, vale and plain,
> And isle and coast, and wide untravers'd main;
> He cast, o'er all, the immeasurable glance,
> And all past views in one broad vision dance.
> Skirting the western heavens and each far pole,
> With blending skies Pacific oceans roll,
> Atlantic surges lead their swelling round,
> And distant straits the polar confines bound.
> The western coasts their long, high summits heave,
> And look majestic o'er the subject wave;
> While, on the lowly east, the winding strand
> Draws from the silent sea and gently steals to land. (146)

Occasionally, Barlow revised a line in order to improve the meter. This eleven-syllable pentameter, "Oh Happy clime! the exulting hero cries," which could have been reduced to ten syllables through elision ("th'exulting") became instead "Oh happy clime! the glad Columbus cries." And, in a similar move from Book Five, this line, "The streams ran purple; all the extended shore" became "The streams ran purple; all the peopled shore."

While Barlow was concerned with stylistic improvement, most of the changes in the fifth edition were made to bring it more into line with Barlow's own changing religious and political ideas. Although not entirely consistent, Barlow deleted most references to Christ and especially to his Christian role as the savior of mankind. Barlow's prose of this period reveals that he had already been substantially influenced by the Deistic doctrines of the European thinkers whose acquaintance he had made; now he was beginning to modify his poem so that it would more accurately reflect his changing ideas. When speaking in Book Seven of the role that religion had played in the development of America, he acknowledged the importance of its moral guidance and its aid to education; but he changed the final couplet from "For this consenting seraphs leave the skies, / The God compassionates, the Saviour dies" (305), to "For this consenting seraphs leave the skies, / Reveal the path of life, and teach them how to rise" (VII, 165–66). Later in the same book, he omitted entirely the line: "Purged from your stains in his atoning blood" (307). And near the end of Book Seven, Barlow eliminated this reference to the "promised Prince" and his second coming:

> Lo, to the cries of grief mild mercy bends,
> Stern vengeance softens and the God descends,
> The atoning God, the pardoning grace to seal,
> The dead to quicken and the sick to heal.
> See from his sacred side the life-blood flow,
> Hear in his groans unutterable woe; . . . (306–7)

Barlow apparently rejected the traditional function that Christ has in the Christian religion and attempted to remove all references to this role in his poem.

By 1793 Barlow had also changed his mind concerning the role that God plays in mankind's progress. The first edition contains many references to God as the source of man's development, a development that demanded little more on man's part than a vague compliance to God's will. The fifth edition, however, reveals Barlow giving more and more responsibility to man; and God takes a secondary and largely passive role, exactly the roles assigned to man and God by the Deists, whom he had rejected in his original plan for the poem. Book One describes God as the source of all good in the following lines deleted from the fifth edition: "From one eternal Spring, what love proceeds! / Smiles in the seraph, in the Saviour bleeds" (129).

As discussed in Chapter 2, Book Eight describes how the excesses of reason and passion can be avoided by following a more moderate path. In the first edition Barlow suggested that this could be achieved by following a bit of advice which, in essence, summarizes standard New Testament theology: "To love the neighbour and adore the God" (333). A small but deft shift in the fifth edition changed the Christian advice to standard Deistic advice: "To love the neighbor, is to please the God" (VIII, 454). The most effective form of worship, Barlow is saying, is to do good to one's fellow man and not to offer formalized adoration.

Barlow also eliminated passages and references to God as the creator of the earth and its inhabitants. Most of these references in the first edition appear to be reflexive acknowledgments of God's presence, as in the account in Book Four of the appearance of the Atlantic coast: "As the glad coast, by Heaven's supreme command, / Won from the waves, presents a new-form'd land" (245). Or, when discussing (in a note to a passage in Book Nine) the importance of commerce in promoting friendly relations among nations, he said: "The spirit of commerce is happily calculated by the Author of wisdom to open an amicable intercourse between all countries . . ." (343). The couplet was dropped entirely in the fifth edition, and the phrase, "by the Author of wisdom," was dropped from the note.

Even when Barlow described man's highest achievement, he deleted a reference to God's part in it. The political development of mankind in *The Vision of Columbus* leads inevitably in Book Nine to the formation of a council of nations to insure man's final perfection. In the first edition, Barlow presented this gathering of nations and acknowledged God's role: "There, hail the splendid seat by Heaven assign'd, / To hear and give the counsels of mankind" (357). These lines were changed in the fifth edition to omit the reference to God as the gathering throng began to "Reach with unwonted speed the place assign'd, / To hear and give the counsels of mankind" (IX, 421–22).

Obviously, Barlow carefully combed his poem for references which placed the responsibility for man's progress on God or religion and eliminated them. In his examination of changes made by Barlow in *The Columbiad*, Leon Howard noted that the plan by which mankind improved was now nature's rather than God's.[3] This change in Barlow's revision of *The Vision of Columbus* can be pushed back at least fourteen years to the publication of the fifth edition in 1793.

Political changes made by Barlow in his fifth edition center almost entirely around his treatment of Louis XVI and around the role that the French monarchy had played in the American Revolution. By 1793 Barlow was a strong supporter of the French Revolution and, in general, of antimonarchy principles. His effusive and servile dedication of the first edition to Louis and his favorable treatment of him in the poem must have been a source of later embarrassment for Barlow. Actually, the dedication had already been dropped for other reasons in the first English edition of 1787, and now Barlow altered Louis' portrait by reinterpreting his motives in aiding the colonists.

Book Six begins in the middle of the Revolutionary War at the point France has formally decided to aid the colonists. The scene shifts from North America to France for a brief description of the French king. In the first edition this account opens with the flattering line "Great Louis there, the pride of monarchs, sate" (279); but the revised version began with a noncommital statement: "Young Bourbon there in sovereign splendor sate" (VI, 5). In addition to this change in Louis' description, Barlow revised his thinking concerning Louis' reasons for entering the war. Originally, he had emphasized the compassion of the French monarch and the clear love of freedom which he had displayed despite his royalty. Since 1787, however, Barlow had gained a more realistic understanding of politics as well as of man. He had been misled and deceived by business associates; he was now living through the turbulent years of the Revolution;

and he had been attacked publicly by English politicians. Now Barlow, a true republican, decided to give the magnanimous motives not to Louis but rather to "unnumber'd sages" and wise counselors of the king who had to persuade Louis to enter the war against his wishes: "By honest guile the royal ear they bend" (VI, 39).

In both editions Louis is given a long speech in which he speaks of freedom, peace, and noble causes; however, in the 1793 edition Barlow revised the two lines introducing the speech, thereby creating a completely different impression. The first edition reads: "O'er all, the approving monarch cast a look, / And listening nations trembled while he spoke" (280). In the fifth edition, "The league propos'd, he lifts his arm to save, / And speaks the borrow'd language of the brave" (VI, 49–50). Louis' speech is reduced to empty rhetoric by the flourish of a couplet. In addition to changing Louis' motives, Barlow also toned down the language which he used to describe the French forces helping the colonists. "Blest Gallia's bands" became "Great Gallia's host" (they were even denied the approval of God), and later a reference to the French was changed from "Great Gallia's line" to "The Gallic line."

A comparison of the first and fifth editions of *The Vision of Columbus* clearly shows, therefore, that Barlow had already begun to make the religious and political changes in his work that are revealed in final form in *The Columbiad.* It is not at all remarkable that Barlow should make these changes at this time because his political prose of 1792 and 1793 reflects the same thinking. What is remarkable is that the changes do not seem to have been noticed before in any detail. The changes in *The Vision of Columbus* described above are the only significant substantive changes made by Barlow; however, he also corrected several typographical errors, doctored a few lines which he thought needed retouching, added explanatory information in a number of footnotes, and revised a few minor details.

Although these changes in the fifth edition were, in summary, significant enough to reveal an alteration in his basic attitudes toward God and King Louis, attitudes that would be strengthened by 1807, the changes themselves were quantitatively very small when compared with the extensive revisions Barlow

made for *The Columbiad*, a poem considerably longer, monu-
mentally more pretentious, and, unfortunately, less successful
than *The Vision of Columbus*. It can be concluded that, because
of the maturity of his ideas and the improvements in the poetry
—primarily by omitting generalized description—Barlow's fifth
edition is his best poetic account of America's past, present,
and future.

II   The Columbiad

Critics have always remarked on the dramatic changes in religious and political thought which they observed in Barlow's
Columbiad. By 1807 Barlow felt no need to keep up the pre-
tense that his poem was simply a series of philosophical ideas
strung together on the framework of a vision. Now, determined
to write an American epic, he changed his title to the more
epical *Columbiad*; added more elaborate epic machinery such as
Hesper, who replaced the anonymous Angel, and Potowmac,
the river god; and charged his diction with more sententious
metaphors, more dignified language, and more outrageous per-
sonifications. Substantively, Barlow added a complete book in
which he gave much more detail of the American Revolution
and the Revolutionary heroes; and he also introduced, in the
same book, the narrative of Lucinda and Heartly, a melodramatic little tale modeled on the captivity stories common to
America for at least one hundred years. The result is a poem,
as others have remarked, considerably longer and infinitely
duller than *The Vision of Columbus* ever was.

Just how seriously Barlow took his role as America's Homer
may be seen in the Preface which preceded the Introduction to
The Columbiad. Barlow is careful to show how each of the
great epic poets of antiquity failed in some way. Homer's *Iliad*
and Virgil's *Aeneid* were excellent poetical structures, but both
failed in the moral object. Of the *Iliad* he said: "Its obvious tendency was to inflame the minds of young readers with an enthusiastic ardor for military fame; to inculcate the pernicious
doctrine of the divine right of kings; to teach both prince and
people that military plunder was the most honorable mode of
acquiring property; and that conquest, violence and war were

the best employment of nations, the most glorious prerogative of bodily strength and of cultivated mind" (378–79).[4] And of the *Aeneid*: "The real design of his poem was to increase the veneration of the people for a master, whoever he might be, and to encourage like Homer the great system of military depredation" (380).

Lucan alone has a moral design that is admirable, but his poetry is weak; the action is rambling and badly arranged. The ideal epic poet, therefore, would combine Homer's poetry with Lucan's morality, and in Barlow's statement of purpose later in the Preface, little doubt is left as to the identity of such an epic poet:

My object is altogether of a moral and political nature. I wish to encourage and strengthen, in the rising generation, a sense of the importance of republican institutions; as being the great foundation of public and private happiness, the necessary aliment of future and permanent meliorations in the condition of human nature. . . .

This is the moment in America to give such a direction to poetry, painting and the other fine arts, that true and useful ideas of glory may be implanted in the minds of men here, to take place of the false and destructive ones that have degraded the species in other countries; impressions which have become so wrought into their most sacred institutions, that it is there thought impious to detect them and dangerous to root them out, tho acknowledged to be false. Wo be to the republican principle and to all the institutions it supports, when once the pernicious doctrine of holiness of error shall creep into the creed of our schools and distort the intellect of our citizens. (389–90)

Both the glorification of America and the blatantly didactic nature of the poem are typical of the poetry being produced in America at this time. In this Preface and in the more extensive notes which Barlow added to his *Columbiad* can be found the suggestion of a critical theory which Barlow hinted at occasionally and which he practiced continuously. If generalizations may be permitted, the poetry of early eighteenth-century America, with its almost exclusive concern for religious themes and with its predominantly Puritan bias, was heavily weighted toward moral instruction and spiritual preparation. Delight in the pleasant appearance of the lines was suspect.[5] By the time Barlow was writing poetry, however, the critical attitudes of the English Augustans were being felt in America. Horace's dictum, to please and instruct, was being followed by many of the poets of the early national period, and the conclusion drawn by the Scottish philosophers that that which is pleasing is also good was, as has been noted earlier, equally accepted.

It was natural, therefore, for Barlow to be concerned with the ornamentation of his poem as well as with the theme, although, throughout, the theme always remained paramount. In his earlier poem, "The Hasty Pudding," when describing the mixing of molasses with his favorite dish, Barlow compared this combination to the productions of poets who "mix . . . the useful with the sweet." And, in a comment facing the first page of his notes to *The Columbiad*, he apologized for having made his notes too long for some tastes and too short for others, saying that his object here as elsewhere was to blend "the useful with the agreeable." For Barlow, the Puritan preoccupation with sin and signs was replaced by a preoccupation with the furtherance of republican principles. Although his poetry was often very didactic, he did quite consciously and openly work at improving the esthetic quality of his poem.

Barlow's liberal social and political concepts, which had already been formed by the 1793 edition, were strengthened in the revisions of *The Columbiad.* The movement away from the reliance on man was made even more emphatic by the specific functions which Barlow gave him. In *The Columbiad*, he enumerated the means by which man could control his own destiny, beginning with the encouragement of industry and trade which would unite man in a common bond of interest. Most of his points can be seen in a hymn to Freedom which Barlow attached to Book Four of *The Columbiad*:

> But when he steps on these regenerate shores,
> His mind unfolding for superior powers,
> FREEDOM, his new Prometheus, here shall rise,
> Light her new torch in my refulgent skies,
> Touch with a stronger life his opening soul,
> Of moral systems fix the central goal,
> Her own resplendent essence. Thence expand
> The rays of reason that illume the land;
> Thence equal rights proceed and equal laws,
> Thence holy Justice all her reverence draws;
> Truth with untarnisht beam descending thence,
> Strikes every eye, and quickens every sense,

Bids bright Instruction spread her ample page,
To drive dark dogmas from the inquiring age,
Ope the true treasures of the earth and skies
And teach the student where his object lies.
    Sun of the moral world! effulgent source
Of man's best wisdom and his steadiest force,
Soul-searching Freedom! here assume thy stand
And radiate hence to every distant land;
Point out and prove how all the scenes of strife,
The shock of states, the impassion'd broils of life,
Spring from unequal sway; and how they fly
Before the splendor of thy peaceful eye;
Unfold at last the genuine social plan,
The mind's full scope, the dignity of man,
Bold nature bursting tho her long disguise
And nations daring to be just and wise.
    Yes! righteous Freedom, heaven and earth and sea
Yield or withold their various gifts for thee;
Protected Industry beneath thy reign
Leads all the virtues in her filial train;
Courageous Probity with brow serene
And Temperance calm presents her placid mien;
Contentment, Moderation, Labor, Art,
Mold the new man and humanize his heart;
To public plenty private ease dilates,
Domestic peace to harmony of states.
Protected Industry, careering far,
Detects the cause and cures the rage of war,
And sweeps with forceful arm to their last graves
Kings from the earth and pirates from the waves. (548–50)

Barlow sees something almost mystical in "these regenerate shores" which will produce freedom which, in turn, will be responsible for the development of a moral world, for industrial progress, and for the humanization of mankind. The implication, however, is that man can bring about these improvements himself; and nowhere does Barlow suggest that faith in God results in moral and social improvement. Politically, man can improve by casting off the vestiges of past enslavement, including, specifically, those left by monarchies and organized religion. Thoughts that Barlow expressed many times in his best prose are summarized here in the final book of *The Columbiad*:

Beneath the footstool all destructive things,
The mask of priesthood and the mace of kings,

> Lie trampled in the dust; for here at last
> Fraud, folly, error all their emblems cast.
> Each envoy here unloads his wearied hand
> Of some old idol from his native land;
> One flings a pagod on the mingled heap,
> One lays a crescent, one a cross to sleep;
> Swords, sceptres, mitres, crowns and globes and stars,
> Codes of false fame and stimulants to wars
> Sink in the settling mass; since guile began,
> These are the agents of the woes of man. (778–79)

Many of the specific revisions that Barlow made in *The Columbiad* reveal his attempt to elevate his diction as he struggled to reach the heights of the Neoclassical genre. *The Vision of Columbus* had begun with a description of Columbus' condition in prison and moved directly into Columbus' soliloquy in which he laments the fact that he will never see America again. *The Columbiad* contains a more formal beginning:

> I sing the Mariner who first unfurl'd
> An eastern banner o'er the western world,
> And taught mankind where future empires lay
> In these fair confines of descending day; . . . (413)

and it contains as well an invocation to Freedom for help in his song:

> Almighty Freedom! give my venturous song
> The force, the charm that to thy voice belong;
> Tis thine to shape my course, to light my way,
> To nerve my country with the patriot lay,
> To teach all men where all their interest lies,
> How rulers may be just and nations wise:
> Strong in thy strength I bend no suppliant knee,
> Invoke no miracle, no Muse but thee. (414)

Only after this formal machinery is presented does Barlow give his account of Columbus in prison.

Another example of Barlow's conscious dignifying of his lines can be found in a Miltonic comparison from *The Vision of Columbus* which was expanded threefold in *The Columbiad.* The comparison is between the development of a common interest out of many individual interests and that of a majestic ocean out of the turbulence of many streams and rivers. *The Vision of Columbus* reads:

As small swift streams their furious course impel,
Til meeting waves their winding currents swell;
Then widening sweep thro' each descending plain,
And move majestic to the boundless main:
'Tis thus society's small sources rise;
Through passions wild their devious progress lies;
Interest and faith and pride and power withstand,
And mutual ills the growing views expand;
Till tribes and states and empires find their place,
And one wide interest sways the peaceful race. (341)

The same comparison in *The Columbiad* is expanded by the addition of numerous details which could, except for their conventionality, increase the effect of the turbulence and the power of the final result; but the implication of the metaphor becomes no clearer; the description merely becomes longer:

As infant streams, from oozing earth at first
With feeble force and lonely murmurs burst,
From myriad unseen fountains draw the rills
And curl contentious round their hundred hills,
Meet, froth and foam, their dashing currents well,
O'er crags and rocks their furious course impel,
Impetuous plunging plough the mounds of earth,
And tear the fostering flanks that gave them birth;
Mad with the strength they gain, they thicken deep
Their muddy waves and slow and sullen creep,
O'erspread whole regions in their lawless pride,
Then stagnate long, then shrink and curb their tide;
Anon more tranquil grown, with steadier sway,
Thro broader banks they shape their seaward way,
From different climes converging, join and spread
Their mingled waters in one widening bed,
Profound, transparent; till the liquid zone
Bands half the globe and drinks the golden sun,
Sweeps onward still the still expanding plain,
And moves majestic to the boundless main.
Tis thus Society's small sources rise;
Thro passions wild her infant progress lies;
Fear, with its host of follies, errors, woes,
Creates her obstacles and forms her foes;
Misguided interest, local pride withstand,
Till long tried ills her growing views expand,
Till tribes and states and empires find their place,
Whose mutual wants her widest walks embrace;
Enlighten'd interest, moral sense at length

> Combine their aids to elevate her strength,
> Lead o'er the world her peace-commanding sway
> And light her steps with everlasting day. (755–57)

Barlow also attempted to heighten the dignity of his epic by increasing his use of personification. During an extended account of a British prison ship, Cruelty is described as a monster-like demon finding delight in the death and disease of the ship:

> She comes, the Fiend! her grinning jaws expand,
> Her brazen eyes cast lightning o'er the strand
> Her wings like thunder-clouds the welkin sweep,
> Brush the tall spires and shade the shuddering deep;
> She gains the deck, displays her wonted shore
> Her cords and scourges wet with prisoner's gore;
> Gripes, pincers, thumb-screws spread beneath her feet;
> Slow poisonous drugs and loads of putrid meat;
> Disease hangs drizzling from her slimy locks,
> And hot contagion issues from her box. (607)

Despite Barlow's desire to produce lines commensurate with the high level of the epic, he succeeded merely, in most cases, in producing a poem that is a bit too pretentious for any age.

The personification of Cruelty comes from Book Six, the only completely new book in the poem and the one in which Barlow expanded his treatment of the American Revolution. While preparing this revision of his poem, Barlow was also attempting to strengthen his country's ties with France rather than with England, whom the Federalists favored. As the prison-ship extract demonstrates, the British were portrayed even more harshly than they had been in the original version of the poem; and, as might be suspected in a poem extolling America's future, the American leaders became even more heroic. Although Barlow differed politically with Washington, he saw him as a symbol of America's future success. In a prophetic moment, Barlow saw a monument being raised to Washington, "A column bold its granite shaft." Throughout this book the battles are described, and the heroes are listed as the war is traced up to the point of France's formal intercession.

In the midst of the Battle of Saratoga, Barlow inserts the story of Lucinda and Heartly, one of his few attempts at extended narrative, and a story dealing with the traditional conflict

between honor and love. Heartly must leave his betrothed in order to answer the call of battle. As he rides off to war, complete
with white plume, Lucinda fears that he may be killed and de-
cides to follow him. Meanwhile, Heartly, fearing for Lucinda's
life, returns and, not finding her, begins his search. Lucinda has
already fallen into the hands of the Mohawks, however, who for
"scalps by British gold are paid." The following passage picks up
the story at this point:

> She starts, with eyes upturn'd and fleeting breath,
> In their raised axes views her instant death,
> Spreads her white hands to heaven in frantic prayer,
> Then runs to grasp their knees, and crouches there.
> Her hair, half lost along the shrubs she past,
> Rolls in loose tangles round her lovely waist;
> Her kerchief torn betrays the globes of snow
> That heave responsive to her weight of woe.
> Does all this eloquence suspend the knife?
> Does no superior tribe contest her life?
> There does: the scalps by British gold are paid;
> A long-hair'd scalp adorns that heavenly head;
> And comes the sacred spoil from friend or foe,
> No marks distinguish, and no man can know.
> With calculating pause and demon grin,
> They seize her hands, and thro her face divine
> Drive the descending ax; the shriek she sent
> Attain'd her lover's ear; he thither bent
> With all the speed his wearied limbs could yield,
> Whirl'd his keen blade and stretcht upon the field
> The yelling fiends; who there disputing stood
> Her gory scalp, their horrid prize of blood.
> He sunk delirious on her lifeless clay
> And past, in starts of sense, the dreadful day. (635–36)

The story is, of course, melodramatic. Barlow attempts to
squeeze every bit of pity out of his reader with bloody details
and with the vivid contrast between the innocence of the victim and the inhuman cruelty of the British-hired murderers,
"and thro her face divine / Drive the descending ax." But Barlow here, as elsewhere in this book of war, is primarily concerned not with thrills and melodrama but rather with demonstrating the horror of war in order to convince people that war
is wrong and that only through peace can man progress. As

discussed previously, Barlow criticized earlier epic poets for presenting war in heroic terms; in Book Six, he attempted to depict the American cause as right, the American leaders as heroic, but war as evil; and the story of Heartly and Lucinda is consistent with this intent.

Barlow introduced several other new subjects into his poem, ones directly related to his emphasis on America's future glory and uniqueness. One of these is his discussion of Negro slavery and its relationship to the American struggle for independence. Near the end of Book Four, Potowmak, the river god, makes a series of predictions including one in which "Old Afric's sons" lose "their shameful fetters." Barlow, however, waited until the beginning of Book Eight before he discussed more fully the shame of slavery in America and the incongruity of having a nation that had just won its freedom holding others in bondage. It is no accident that Barlow placed this passage immediately after the account of the American Revolution and in the middle of his hymn to peace. Masters and slaves are uncomfortably close parallels to kings and servants; they both spring from the same distorted view of man. In a Popean couplet, Barlow summarizes his attitude: "Ah! would you not be slaves, with lords and kings,/Then be not masters; there the danger springs" (697).

The danger of slavery is the possible destruction of America. Atlas, guardian of Africa, forecasts the overwhelming results of continued slavery in a passage that might be taken as a prediction of the Civil War:

> Nor shall these pangs atone the nation's crime;
> Far heavier vengeance, in the march of time,
> Attends them still; if still they dare debase
> And hold inthrall'd the millions of my race;
> A vengeance that shall shake the world's deep frame,
> That heaven abhors, and hell might shrink to name.
> Nature, long outraged, delves the crusted sphere
> And molds the mining mischief dark and drear;
> Europa too the penal shock shall find,
> The rude soul-selling monsters of mankind. (693)

Before leaving the subject of slavery, Barlow carefully points out, as always, that Europe and particularly England was responsible for bringing this evil to the virgin American territory:

> Too much of Europe, here transplanted o'er,
> Nursed feudal feeling on your tented shore,
> Brought sable serfs from Afric, call'd it gain,
> And urged your sires to forge the fatal chain. (698)

America has broken almost completely with the feudal institutions of Europe, but one more remains to be broken:

> Complete their triumph, fix their firm abode,
> Purge all privations from your liberal code,
> Restore their souls to men, give earth repose
> And save your sons from slavery, wars and woes. (699)

As America threw off its political master, so should it purge itself of the slave system. Complete freedom is not possible until both slaves and masters have been eliminated.

Permeating *The Columbiad*, of course, is the period's almost hysterical desire to sever as many Old World ties as possible. Although, in practice, America remained an integral part of the Western world and in many ways was an extension of England, its people cried out, nevertheless, for a literary, social, and economic independence to supplement their political independence. One of the less significant of these drives for separation might be called a desire for "orthographical independence." Barlow's former classmate and former friend, Noah Webster, America's guardian of its language, had been urging Americans to adopt simpler, more uniform, and more uniquely American spelling practices, and, by 1807, Barlow agreed with him.

A number of spelling changes were made in the first edition of *The Columbiad*; however, it was in the 1808 second edition that Barlow incorporated most of the orthographical reform that characterized *The Columbiad*. Although unpublished letters in the Harvard University Library reveal that Barlow consulted Webster on questions of spelling and the use of foreign words, Barlow had long been interested in language and language changes.[6] It is safe to assume, therefore, that Barlow's Postscript to his poem, which comments on language and describes spelling reforms incorporated into the poem, was largely the product of Barlow's own thinking supported by the authority of Noah Webster.

Among the changes in spelling suggested by Barlow were

dropping the *u* in words such as *labour* and *honour*, reducing *though* and *through* to *tho* and *thro*, and changing the final *ed* of past tense verbs to *t* as in *perisht* and *astonisht* "because it brings a numerous class of words to be written as they are spoken." Running throughout Barlow's suggestions is the concept of language as a changing, growing phenomenon: "The idea of putting a stop to innovation in a living language is absurd, unless we put a stop to thinking. When a language becomes fixt it becomes a dead language. Men must leave it for a living one, in which they can express their ideas with all their changes, extensions and corrections. The duty of the critic in this case is only to keep a steady watch over the innovations that are offered, and require a rigid conformity to the general principles of idiom . . ." (856).

In language, as in social and political history, Barlow believed in progress. The idea of a Golden Age, he said in one of his notes, is dangerous because if man ever feels he has reached perfection, he will cease to strive. As did Goethe, Barlow saw the danger of satisfaction. *The Columbiad* is the vision of that earthly improvement, but the emphasis is always on the pursuit of that perfection in America's present.

Any assessment of *The Columbiad* must begin with the realization that it need never have been written. The only improvement over the first edition of *The Vision of Columbus* is in the clarification and maturation of the philosophical and political concepts on which the poem is based, as has been pointed out by Leon Howard;[7] and these ideas were added to the revised 1793 fifth edition. Almost all other additions and changes were detrimental. Here as elsewhere in Barlow's poetry, when he was most conscious of being a poet, he wrote his worst poetry. It is rather in his short, unpretentious pieces that he contributed most significantly to the poetry of the early national period; and for these works he should be primarily remembered as a poet.

CHAPTER 4

Poet of Corn-Meal Mush

BARLOW DEVOTED most of his literary efforts before 1787 to his long, philosophical poem, *The Vision of Columbus*; between 1787 and 1800 to pamphlet warfare on both sides of the Atlantic; and from 1800 until his death to statesman-like prose works and to a final revision of his *Vision, The Columbiad.* During his lifetime, he also composed, as stated earlier, numerous short poems ranging from early Cavalier imitations to his final bitter outburst against Napoleon and from very self-conscious expressions of American promise to a mock-heroic treatment of corn-meal mush. In addition, he composed wedding-anniversary poems intended only for his wife, Ruth, and occasional New Year poems to be published in the *American Mercury*, poems which Zunder terms frankly "potboilers."[1]

The vast majority of these poems are best left to obscurity; several, however, are worth examining for historical or biographical relevancies; and at least two are among the best poems produced during this period and are worth more than all the lines found in *The Vision of Columbus* and *The Columbiad.* These are "The Hasty Pudding" and "Advice to a Raven in Russia," the former not published until two years after it was written and the latter not published until 1938.[2]

Theodore Zunder in his examination of Barlow up to the publication of *The Vision* summarized his poetry of this early period: "The creative power of Barlow was obviously shackled by convention in diction. Neither the Romantic Movement nor association with continental men of letters freed his style nor pointed out fresh subject-matter for poems."[3] The statement is true, but it also applies to all other poets of the time. Even Philip Freneau, who was exploring the possibility of American subject matter, continued to use the forms favored by the Augustans; for the American Revolution in versification did not come for another half-century.

Several poems may serve as examples of Barlow's occasional verse. The first is a poem which Barlow sent to Elisha Babcock of the *American Mercury* (the newspaper which Barlow and Babcock had founded) to be published as the New Year's poem for 1806. Although the poem apparently was never published, it is typical of the conventional newsboy's greeting to his customers and also represents an exaggerated seriousness and a mock-heroic tone which Barlow used elsewhere, notably in "The Hasty Pudding."

> While you, my kind customer, smoke your cigars,
> And talk at safe distance of earthquakes & wars,
> Napoleon, Vesuvius, alternately raging,
> And Keisers & Czars who have caught the contagion,
> Behold your poor post-boy, whose feet never fail
> To bring the good journal that tells you the tale.
>   I've serv'd up the dishes on which you've been treated
> Your fine Indian treaties, your Bashaws defeated,
> Our friends coming home to their sweethearts & wives,
> When you knock'd off their fetters & rescued their lives.
> As soon as the Dons recommenced their vacations,
> And John Bull insulted the rights of all nations,
> While France took ambassadors prisoners of state,
> Or Turks kill'd the Jews for to plunder their plate,
> The facts I collected & laid them before ye;
> My duty was done when I'd told you the story.
>   I still shall continue, as well as I'm able,
> To furnish deserts for each citizen's table;
> I'll follow three emperors thro' their wild rambles,
> Count the two-legged cattle that fill their great shambles,
> Rehearse all their battles as fast as they fight'em;
> So that when they go wrong you can mend'em and right'em;
> And when we've a pause with those quarrelsome elves,
> You may learn from my sheets what you're doing yourselves,
> For I know very well how to echo my betters,
> Repeat your long speeches, long motions, long letters;
> And tho' afar off they should never be known,
> Each eloquent wight will at least read his own.
> I hope they will turn upon matters of weight,
> How to make all your fortunes, & build up the state.
> One thing I forgot tho'; but since I am here
> I'll add it,—I WISH YOU A HAPPY NEW YEAR.[4]

Barlow's short poems to his wife to celebrate the anniversary of their wedding range from very stilted and formal compositions, such as the poem for 1793 which begins, "Blest Hymen, hail that memorable day / Whose twelfth [*sic*] return my constant bosom warms,"[5] to less pretentious compositions suggesting in dilution the light tone of the Cavalier poets, as in the following poem inscribed "To my wife, on the anniversary of our wedding, 26th January, 1800":

> If nineteen years of marriage ties
>   Can make me love so strong,
> Pray tell how high the flames will rise
>   When nourished twice as long.
>
> For nourishment, like what you give,
>   So sweet, so wholesome too,
> Will bid the torch forever live,
>   And live alone for you.[6]

Another poem written by Barlow for a specific occasion reveals the pomposity and bombast to which he reverts when self-consciously dignified. This ten-line elegy was written in June, 1802, to comfort the grieving mother of Charlotte Villette, a sixteen-year-old girl:

> Could youth, could innocence, could beauty save,
> Our Charlotte sure had found a later grave,
> But, hapless mother, cease! Your tears but show
> The poor scant measure of our common woe;
> Ah cease that vulgar grief, & dare to find
> A tribute worthier her exalted mind;
> Resume her virtues that you planted there,
> Reclaim that merit, none with you can share;
> Reclaim her force of thought, her vermil hue,
> Your friends demand her promised life in you.[7]

I Commencement Poems

The final examples of Barlow's early occasional poetry were written for public presentation and were intended as serious pronouncements; and the occasion for both was a Yale College commencement. The first poem, "The Prospect of Peace," was delivered on July 23, 1778, when Barlow received his bachelor's degree; the second, "A Poem Spoken at the Public Commencement at Yale College, in New Haven, September 12, 1781," was delivered when Barlow received a master's. Both poems are typical of the many patriotic outbursts of this period, and both reflect the ideas which Barlow was putting into his *Vision of Columbus.* In fact, the second poem was composed largely of portions written for inclusion in Barlow's longer poem.

Although Barlow did not begin *The Vision of Columbus* until the following year, he clearly used ideas in "The Prospect of Peace" that showed up later in his *Vision.* His Protestantism was even more orthodox at this time than it was in the longer poem, as might be expected. Near the end of the poem he speaks of the millennium in strictly Christian terms, as the establishment of God's kingdom on this earth:

> As when th'asterial blaze o'er Bethl'em stood,
> Which mark'd the birth-place of th'incarnate God;
> When eastern priests the heavenly splendor view'd,
> And numerous crouds the wonderous sign pursu'd;
> So eastern kings shall view th'unclouded day
> Rise in the West and streak its golden way;
> *That* signal spoke a Saviour's humble birth,
> *This* speaks his long and glorious reign on earth! (11)

Earlier in the poem he had said, "Here the pure Church, Descending from her God, / Shall fix on earth her long and last abode"; Barlow was taking no chances before this Yale gathering.

Most of the poem is concerned with the vision which the goddess Peace presents. The order of the details of this vision closely parallels the sequence of events presented to Columbus in Book Seven of *The Vision of Columbus*, a sequence based upon the chronological development of the various concerns of a developing country. In the Argument for Book Seven, the list is: "Hymn to Peace. Progress of Arts in America. Fur-trade. Fisheries. Productions and Commerce. Education. Philosophical Inventions. Painting. Poetry" (298). The vision of "The Prospect of Peace" comprises a similar listing. After a reference to "god-like senate," Barlow discusses in turn the harvest and the commerce that a young country needs for survival, followed by the development of science and learning, and finally the flowering of the "blest Muses": "Unnumber'd bards shall string the heavenly lyre, / To those blest strains which heavenly themes inspire" (9). The poem closes with a generalized view of the millennium, a combination of vague optimism and Protestant certainty:

> Then Love shall rule, and Innocence adore,
> Discord shall cease, and Tyrants be no more;
> 'Till yon bright orb, and those celestial spheres,
> In radiant circles, mark a thousand years;
> 'Till the grand *fiat* burst th'etherial frames—
> Worlds crush on worlds, and Nature sink in flames!
> The Church elect, from smouldering ruins, rise,
> And sail triumphant thro' the yielding skies,
> Hail'd by the Bridegroom! to the Father given,
> The Joy of Angels, and the Queen of Heaven! (11–12)

The reference to lovers ruling the earth suggests Barlow's description of the unifying force within the universe, which he presented at the end of Book Eight of *The Vision* as "The attracting force of universal love."

Barlow's commencement poem for 1781 also concludes with a reference to the power of love as the instrument for man's progress. Again, with the support of an "inspiring God" and this time accompanied by the songs of the poet, men will be "Lind'd in the chain of harmonizing love" and proceed to "their kindred mansions in the skies." "Poem Spoken at the Public Commencement at Yale College" is presented also in the form of a vision. After an opening section lamenting the seven years of war and the threat that this poses to Yale and to learning in general, the poet, while wandering through a "gloomy grove," sees a form take shape before him. The description of "Learning's bright Genius" illustrates the use Barlow made of material from his *Vision of Columbus*. The following passage from the commencement poem describes the form:

> Now a calm splendor burst the saddening gloom,
> And gales etherial breath'd a glad perfume,
> Mild in the midst a form celestial shone,
> Rob'd in the vestments of the rising sun;
> Tall rose his stature, dignity and grace
> Mov'd in his limbs and wanton'd in his face,
> His folding mantle flow'd in easy pride,
> His harp divine lay useless by his side,

> His locks in curls from myrtle chaplets hung
> And sounds melodious melted from his tongue. (31–32)

Book One of *The Vision of Columbus* describes the Angel as it first appeared to Columbus, who is also discouraged:

> The growing splendor fill'd the astonish'd room,
> And gales etherial breath'd a glad perfume;
> Mile in the midst a radiant seraph shone,
> Robed in the vestments of the rising sun;
> Tall rose his stature, youth's primeval grace
> Moved o'er his limbs and wanton'd in his face,
> His closing wings, in golden plumage drest,
> With gentle sweep came folding o'er his breast,
> His locks in rolling ringlets glittering hung,
> And sounds melodious moved his heavenly tongue. (128)

The remainder of the poem is devoted, through visions and the words of the celestial form, to showing that Learning has not abandoned mankind in much the same way that the Angel assured Columbus that his efforts were not wasted.

Barlow first described the New World's geographical expanse in a passage later incorporated in revised form into *The Vision of Columbus*:

> Where the deep gulph unfolds Floridia's shore,
> To where Ontario bids hoarse Laurence roar;
> Where Missisippi's waves their sources boast,
> Where groves and floods and realms and climes are lost,
> To where the mild Atlantic's length'ning tide,
> Laves numerous towns, and swells their naval pride.
> And see! by nature's hand o'er all bestow'd,
> The last pure polish of the forming God.
> What various grandeur strikes the gladdening eyes!
> Bays stretch their arms and mountains lift the skies;
> The lakes, unfolding, point the streams their way,
> The plains, the hills their lengthening skirts display,
> The vales draw forth, fair wave the glimmering wilds,
> And all the majesty of nature smiles. (33)

On this new land will develop a society superior to any the world has yet produced. As in *The Vision*, this society will reach a state of eternal peace not so much by man's efforts as by the inevitability of progress itself working within God's universe. Throughout the following passage may be seen a larger, external plan at work:

> Yet thro' the whole the same progressive plan,
> Which draws, for mutual succour, man to man,
> From men to tribes, from tribes to nations spreads,
> And private ties to public compact leads,
> Shall rise by slow degrees, and still extend,
> Their power their interest and their passions blend,
> Their wars grow milder, policies enlarge,
> Increasing nations feel the general charge,
> Form broad alliances for mutual aid,
> Mingle their manners and extend their trade,
> Till each remotest realm, by friendship join'd,
> Link in the chain and harmonize mankind,
> The union'd banner be at last unfurl'd,
> And wave triumphant round the accordant world. (34–35)

This view is comparable to the vision of man's progress given to Columbus by the Angel in Book Nine of *The Vision of Columbus.*

At this point in the poem, Barlow introduces a series of more specific present and future glories—as he did in "The Prospect of Peace" and as he was to do in *The Vision*—that move in a roughly chronological order from the early discovery and settlement of the country, through the practical concerns of establishing a society, to the fine arts, society's crowning achievement. After references to architecture, landscaping, painting, sculpture, and music, Barlow discusses briefly the poet and his function in society. The poet of the future will discuss "Virtues and loves and heavenly themes" rather than the accounts of war, death, and destruction which occupied the older writers, particularly of the epic, that highest form of all poetry. With concealed immodesty, Barlow was praising exactly the kind of poem he himself was then writing. In fairness to Barlow, it should be mentioned that most poets who also make critical statements display a close and understandable similarity between their poetry and their criticism.

The poet in Barlow's commencement poem assumes a much more dominant role in the development of society and in the recording of this development. Whereas God and his church usher in the millennium in "The Prospect of Peace," perfection

is reached here through a combination of God and "peace inspiring song." In fact, the final point that Barlow makes is that
the poet's "lays on earth prelude the heavenly song." The Cal-
vinist concept of this life as a preparation for the next one has
been transformed by Barlow into a critical statement which
could offend neither the Calvinists nor the poets in his audience.

II   *"Elegy on Titus Hosmer"*

When Barlow expressed regret in his commencement poem
over the misfortune that had befallen his country and particularly Yale, one of the specific losses he mentioned was the
death of Titus Hosmer, a judge and a representative from Connecticut to the Continental Congress. Hosmer had encouraged
Barlow during the early stages of the planning of his *Vision of
Columbus*, and Barlow repaid him after his death in 1780 with a
poetic tribute. "An Elegy on the Late Honorable Titus Hosmer,"
published in 1781, reflects a genuineness of emotion in spite of
the conventionalized diction and imagery. The poem is interesting primarily because of the way it combines the conventions
of the traditional pastoral elegy with references to conditions in
America and to the grief of Hosmer's wife and family.

The poem begins with a standard invocation asking for the
skill to be worthy of the subject. However, instead of appealing
to the muse of some other source of inspiration, Barlow has "the
orphan'd Muse" appeal to Hosmer for help much as Barlow had
earlier appealed to Hosmer. In an attempt to convince Hosmer
that he should return, Barlow reminds him of those he has left
behind, thus providing the Procession of Mourners. Among
these mourners are the poet himself, the worthies of the Congress, and his wife and children, who are compared to Cynthia,
the moon, and the planets seeking "their sire the sun." The sun,
which returns each day and also ushers in the spring only reminds the poet that Hosmer will not return. Hosmer is then en-
treated to interfere in behalf of his country or, if this is impossible, to give a vision of America's future greatness. Surprisingly,
Barlow ignores the opportunity to provide his public with another view of the future; instead, he lists Hosmer's accomplishments and ends with a plea that Hosmer at least drop his mantle

from heaven to one who could take his place. The Consolation is achieved by the realization that Hosmer in heaven will be comforted and pleased by the progress of America and by the spreading of American ideas throughout the world, a realization which also serves to comfort the grieving family to whom the final portion of the poem is directed.

Barlow's poem is too filled with the self-conscious rhetoric of the elegiac tradition. Instead of allowing the conventional form of the pastoral elegy to serve as a control over emotion, Barlow seems to be making excuses so he can fit in these conventions. Instead of raising the death of an individual to more universal significances, thereby developing a serious thematic statement, Barlow uses the death of Hosmer to exalt Hosmer and to make some vague statements about America's future. Nevertheless, Barlow was striving quite consciously to unite his patriotic theme with an accepted poetic form, to adapt a convention of Western poetry to the American poetic scene.

III   *"The Conspiracy of Kings"*

In 1792 Barlow turned to another form of poetry, verse satire, modeled, he thought, on the Classical satires of Juvenal and on the more recent ones of Pope. At this time Barlow was freely sharing his opinions with anyone who would listen. Several weeks after publishing *Advice to the Privileged Orders*, a reasoned and reasonable political pamphlet, Barlow produced "The Conspiracy of Kings: A Poem Addressed to the Inhabitants of Europe, from Another Quarter of the World." Contrary to what Barlow and his critics insist, the poem is not a satire; for it has none of the traditional satiric devices. The only exaggeration involved is in the bitterness of the attack. Indeed, the poem is rather a direct and vituperative name-calling broadside against the European monarchies who were uniting to oppose the French Republic at this time and against Edmund Burke, a favorite target of the English and French liberals. Of the kings he says:

> Drones of the church and harpies of the state,—
> Ye, whose curst sires, for blood and plunder fam'd
> Sultans or kings or czars or emp'rors nam'd,

> Taught the deluded world their claims to own,
> And raise the crested reptiles to a throne,– (69)

And of Burke: "Oh Burke, degenerate slave! with grief and shame / The Muse indignant must repeat thy name" (75). All the political, social, moral, and economic evils of the world are attributed to these monarchs and their supporters:

> 'Tis Rank, Distinction, all the hell that springs
> From those prolific monsters, Courts and Kings.
> These are the vampires nurs'd on nature's spoils;
> For these with pangs the starving peasant toils, . . . (80)

Barlow, who concludes his poem with some advice to these rulers, urges them to throw off the unnatural designation of king and "Hail MAN, exalted title! first and blest"; and, as usual, he moves finally to a view of man's future:

> Behold th'ascending bliss that waits your call,
> Heav'n's own bequest, the heritage of all.
> Awake to wisdom, seize the proffer'd prize;
> From shade to light, from grief to glory rise.
> Freedom at last, with reason in her train,
> Extends o'er earth her everlasting reign; . . . (82)

The petty tone and lack of reasoned support which characterize "The Conspiracy of Kings" contrast dramatically with the rationality and statesmanlike dignity of his *Advice*; and the heavy-handed "satire" of this poem contrasts just as dramatically with the whimsical tone of Barlow's most successful and least self-conscious poem, "The Hasty Pudding: A Poem in Three Cantoes. Written in Chambéry, in Savoy, January, 1793." Ironically, this poem is successful because it mocks those very epic conventions which Barlow used all too seriously in his vision poems. Exaggerated for the sake of humor, these conventions are often delightful; exaggerated for the sake of dignity, they are deadly.

IV   *"The Hasty Pudding"*

The year 1792 had been an exhilarating one for Joel Barlow, but also a wearying one. Giving advice to the world and campaigning unsuccessfully for a seat in the National Convention from Savoy had temporarily tired him and had caused his mind to return to his early days in the Connecticut hills. While in this relaxed and contemplative mood at an inn in Chambéry, he was unexpectedly served a dish of corn-meal mush, known to New Englanders as hasty pudding. His reminiscences and relaxed mood combined to produce a 375-line mock-heroic and mock-pastoral poem, which traces this New England favorite from the growing of the corn by an Indian maid to the instructions in etiquette which accompany its use.

Barlow begins his poem by consciously rejecting the political, visionary poetry he had been writing and by turning instead to "A softer theme," "A virgin theme," yet one "well-suited to inspire / The purest frenzy of poetic fire." In true pastoral fashion Barlow calls upon the Muse for poetic inspiration, insisting upon his own inadequacy. The diction is intentionally inflated, and the Muse is hasty pudding:

> Oh! could the smooth, the emblematic song
> Flow like the genial juices o'er my tongue,
> Could those mild morsels in my numbers chime,
> And, as they roll in substance, roll in rhyme,
> No more thy aukward unpoetic name
> Should shun the muse or prejudice thy fame;
> But rising grateful to the accustom'd ear,
> All bards should catch it, and all realms revere! (88)

After dedicating his poem to the unknown Indian maid who "first learned with stones to crack the well-dried maize" and fashioned this pudding, and after discussing the names given to this dish by the various countries, the poet concludes that his own New England name describes it most accurately for reasons passed on to him by his father:

> In *haste* the boiling caldron o'er the blaze,
> Receives and cooks the ready-powder'd maize;
> In *haste* 'tis serv'd, and then in equal *haste*,
> With cooling milk, we make the sweet repast.
> No carving to be done, no knife to grate
> The tender ear, and wound the stony plate;
> But the smooth spoon, just fitted to the lip,
> And taught with art the yielding mass to dip,

By frequent Journies to the bowl well stor'd,
Performs the hasty honors of the board." (90)

Canto One ends with a catalogue of several favorite American meals which the poet admits are tempting but which he finally rejects because "To that loved bowl my spoon by instinct flies."

In Canto Two Barlow acknowledges the necessity of rules even for a naturally good dish such as hasty pudding,[8] which combines the New England virtue of plainness with the democratic virtue of equality. (It "cheers alike the servant and the lord.") The remainder of the poem presents these rules for growing, preparing, serving, and eating the dish as well as introducing several short digressions. Barlow's account of the cornstalks breaking through the ground and reaching rapidly skyward is amusingly presented because of the elaborate epic description which accompanies the account:

Slow springs the blade, which check'd by chilling rains,
Ere yet the sun the seat of Cancer gains;
But when his fiercest fires emblaze the land,
Then start the juices, then the roots expand;
Then, like a column of Corinthian mould,
The stalk struts upward, and the leaves unfold;
The busy branches all the ridges fill,
Entwine their arms, and kiss from hill to hill.
Here cease to vex them; all your cares are done;
Leave the last labours to the parent sun;
Beneath his genial smiles, the well-drest field,
When autumn calls, a plenteous crop shall yield. (94)

Turgidity, of course, was no stranger to Barlow. When used in *The Vision of Columbus* or, even more disastrously, in *The Columbiad*, it puffed up trivialities to the point of absurdity. In "The Hasty Pudding," however, Barlow was in complete control of the overstatement, making it possible for him to create the humor and at the same time insist on the significance of the action. Within the context of the poem, the corn is still important even though Barlow is mildly and good-naturedly poking fun at his own description. In "The Hasty Pudding" he always goes just this far in his bombast and no further.

While the preceding section makes use of epic descriptions, the following one is definitely pastoral. In it the maid and swain meet secretly beneath the overtowering cornstalks:

> Now the strong foliage bears the standards high,
> And shoots the tall top-gallants to the sky;
> The suckling ears their silky fringes bend,
> And pregnant grown, their swelling coats distend;
> The loaded stalk, while still the burden grows,
> O'erhangs the space that runs between the rows;
> High as a hop-field waves the silent grove,
> A safe retreat for little thefts of love,
> When the pledged roasting-ears invite the maid,
> To meet her swain beneath the new form'd shade;
> His generous hand unloads the cumbrous hill,
> And the green spoils her ready basket fill;
> Small compensation for the twofold bliss,
> The promised wedding and the present kiss. (94)

The fullness of the grain and the ripeness of the earth in spring-time are underscored by the traditional lovers with their promise of marriage and prospects for parenthood.

Canto Three is the most amusing section of the poem because of its emphasis on the rules which govern the preparation and consumption of the pudding. Barlow manages to combine the rules for husking corn with the traditional husking bee of rural America. The result is a parody of the games found in epic poetry as well as a bit of American local color:

> The laws of Husking ev'ry wight can tell;
> And sure no laws he ever keeps so well:
> For each red ear a general kiss he gains,
> With each smut ear she smuts the luckless swains;
> But when to some sweet maid a prize is cast,
> Red as her lips and taper as her waist,
> She walks the round, and culls one favor'd beau,
> Who leaps, the luscious tribute to bestow.
> Various the sport, as are the wits and brains
> Of well pleas'd lasses and contending swains;
> Till the vast mound of corn is swept away,
> And he that gets the last ear wins the day. (96)

In the midst of the preparation for the feast, another standard element of the epic, Barlow inserts an amusing apostrophe to the cow because this animal provides milk, the final touch needed for eating the pudding:

> Blest cow! thy praise shall still my notes employ,
> Great source of health, the only source of joy;

> How oft thy teats these pious hands have prest!
> How oft thy bounties proved my only feast!
> How oft I've fed thee with my fav'rite grain!
> And roar'd, like thee, to see thy children slain!
>   Ye swains who know her various worth to prize,
> Ah! house her well from Winter's angry skies.
> Potatoes, pumpkins, should her sadness cheer,
> Corn from your crib, and mashes from your beer;
> When Spring returns she'll well acquit the loan,
> And nurse at once your infants and her own. (97)

Both the diction and syntax are overly ornate and, even for Barlow, too artificially wrought. The apostrophe could almost be mistaken for a parody of Barlow's description of Washington in Book Five of *The Columbiad*.

The remainder of the poem details first the preparation of the pudding:

> First in your bowl the milk abundant take,
> Then drop with care along the silver lake
> Your flakes of pudding; these at first will hide
> Their little bulk beneath the swelling tide;
> But when their growing mass no more can sink,
> When the soft island looms above the brink,
> Then check your hand; you've got the portion's due;
> So taught our sires, and what they taught is true. (97–98)

And, finally, Barlow presents a short masterpiece in trivia when the choice of spoons is discussed as though Barlow were describing an important scientific experiment or the selection of an instrument of war:

> There is a choice in spoons. Though small appear
> The nice distinction, yet to me 'tis clear.
> The deep bowl'd Gallic spoon, contrived to scoop
> In ample draughts the thin diluted soup,
> Performs not well in those substantial things,
> Whose mass adhesive to the metal clings;
> Where the strong labial muscles must embrace,
> The gentle curve, and sweep the hollow space.
> With ease to enter and discharge the freight,
> A bowl less concave but still more dilate,
> Becomes the pudding best. The shape, the size,
> A secret rests unknown to vulgar eyes.
> Experienc'd feeders can alone impart

> A rule so much above the lore of art.
> These tuneful lips, that thousand spoons have tried,
> With just precision could the point decide,
> Tho' not in song; the muse but poorly shines
> In cones, and cubes, and geometric lines;
> Yet the true form, as near as she can tell,
> Is that small section of a goose-egg shell,
> Which in two equal portions shall divide
> The distance from the centre to the side. (98)

The incongruity between the subject and the description produces the humor here as it does throughout the poem.

Part of the success of the poem is due to the tight unity which Barlow manages to maintain, a unity which is generally missing in his other poetry. The single object of hasty pudding, of course, makes this possible; but Barlow also avoids the possibility of long digressions. The digressions which do exist rarely go beyond a one- or two-line aphorism as, for instance, when early in the poem, Barlow tells what his poem is not about: "Ye Gallic flags, that o'er their heights unfurled, / Bear death to kings and freedom to the world, / I sing not you." And, thus, he makes a flattering reference to the French. In Canto Three, the poet is considering the variety of ways in which hasty pudding may be served. One of these ways, with molasses, allows the user to "mix, like bards, the useful with the sweet." The literary theory implied here is one which Barlow tried to follow but one in which he was only too infrequently successful. "The Hasty Pudding" is one poem in which he was successful.

The poem is actually divided into two distinct parts, the first canto relating preliminary information such as praise for the dish, its origin, and its relative superiority to other dishes, and the last two cantos describing the actual preparation and consumption of the pudding. One unifying principle, in addition to the obvious one of a single subject, unites the two parts, and several smaller principles provide a tight organization for the last two cantos. In a sense, Barlow moves rapidly from the dawn of civilization to the sophisticated manners of a highly cultured civilization; and, in doing so, he achieves, through the contrast, a light degree of satiric undertone. In Canto One, he conjectures on the unknown Indian maid who first prepared this meal, "some tawny Ceres," or perhaps even Oella, the Peruvian queen of his own *The Vision of Columbus.* The concluding short section of the poem then describes in overly rational fashion how the pudding might be eaten without spilling it:

> Fear not to slaver; 'tis no deadly sin.
> Like the free Frenchman, from your joyous chin
> Suspend the ready napkin; or, like me,
> Poise with one hand your bowl upon your knee;
> Just in the zenith your wise head project,
> Your full spoon, rising in a line direct,
> Bold as a bucket, heeds no drops that fall,
> The wide mouth'd bowl will surely catch them all. (98)

This section not only completes the progress from the primitive to the cultured; it also pokes a bit of fun at the result of this progress but does so completely without bitterness and without being too serious about it.

Within the organization of the second and third cantos, at least two closely related unifying principles are used. The first one is the simple fact that Barlow follows the movement of hasty pudding from the planting of the grain to its consumption, including in this development more specific details than he used anywhere else in his poetry, details that might be called "local color." The second unifying element is the conventional cycle of the seasons, which conveniently parallels the growing, preparation, and eating of the meal. Barlow is careful to point out the particular time of the year when these various activities take place. After a preliminary discussion of the necessity of rules for the preparation of the meal, the poet refers to that time of year "When now the ox, obedient to thy call, / Repays the loan that fill'd the winter stall" (93). The corn is planted and begins to break through the ground "Ere yet the sun the seat of Cancer gains." After a season of growing, the harvest is described: "At last the closing season browns the plain, / And ripe October gathers in the grain" (95). Canto Three begins: "The days grow short"; and then comes the description of the husking bee, the feasting, and the discussion of how the pudding should be eaten.

The basic movement of the poem is forward, toward civilization, toward harvest, toward eating this New England delicacy. This forward movement is characteristic of almost everything

Barlow wrote as he foresaw something better for the future. The difference in "The Hasty Pudding" is that Barlow was actually recalling his past, not predicting the future; and he was doing so in a nostalgic mood, not with the millennial fever that usually accompanied his writing.

Much of the success of this poem is due to the tight organization and the humor produced by the incongruity between the subject and method of the poem; but another ingredient plays an equally important part. The heroic couplet is used with a variety and a subtlety here that is unfortunately missing in Barlow's more serious verse; in fact, much of the informality and playfulness of the poem is the result of Barlow's manipulation of the couplet. At times, the balance and symmetry of the lines are almost excruciating as a trivial subject is described as though it were momentous. For instance, in the following lines, the boys and girls are taking their places around a table in preparation for the husking bee:

> Where the huge leap lies center'd in the hall,
> The lamp suspended from the cheerful wall,
> Brown corn-fed nymphs, and strong hard-handed beaux,
> Alternate rang'd, extend in circling rows,
> Assume their seats, the solid mass attack;
> The dry husks rustle, and the corn-cobs crack;
> The son, the laugh, alternate notes resound,
> And the sweet cider trips in silence round. (96)

The extreme regularity of the caesura placement in lines two to six and the syntactical balance of the two halves of the lines suggest a vigorous preparation for a significant event. Instead of producing this event, however, Barlow breaks the balanced phrasing by a reference to the cider making the rounds of the table and then, in the next section, concludes the description of the husking bee.

Not all of the poem, however, makes use of the very formal structural possibilities of the couplet. Barlow often uses a more conversational syntax, a greater variety of caesura placements, and more enjambement to produce poetry which is relaxed and informal, entirely in keeping with the pace of life which he is recalling. A good example of this is the passage quoted earlier in which the poet recalls his father's account of how hasty pudding received its name.

Van Wyck Brooks's statement that "The Hasty Pudding" is Barlow's "best and one of the first good American poems"[9] is representative of the comments made about this poem by the critics. They refer to its freshness and humor and call it best because it lacks the stilted pomposity of Barlow's other poetry, but the poem is successful also for the skillful way in which Barlow used his materials. The poem succeeds not only by default.

V   *"Advice to a Raven in Russia"*

Leon Howard has said that "The Hasty Pudding" reflects a Wordsworthian experience, "an overflow of whimsicality rather than of powerful feeling,"[10] recollected in a state of tranquility. If "The Hasty Pudding" is an overflow of whimsicality, then Barlow's last poem, "To a Raven in Russia," is certainly an outburst of powerful feeling recollected not in tranquility but shouted in the midst of an agonizing moment. This poem is completely unlike anything else Barlow wrote, for the sheer power of the emotion carries it beyond the conscious modeling and conversational rhetoric that marks his other poetry, even "The Hasty Pudding." In a very real sense, "Advice to a Raven in Russia" is a cry from hell.

The hell of Barlow's poem is the Europe that Napoleon in his madness had created. As has already been related in Chapter 1, Barlow, hoping to conclude a treaty with France, had followed the French as far as Poland in its invasion of Russia. During the winter of 1812 Napoleon's advance was checked, and his planned, orderly retreat turned into a complete rout with many thousands dying of exhaustion, starvation, and exposure along the road that Barlow and his young nephew, Thomas, traveled. The desperation and desolation of the countryside were only hinted at during this flight in the letters Thomas Barlow wrote to Miss Clara, Ruth Barlow's sister; for a letter dated December 17 reads in part: "The late battles near the Beresina have been very bloody; nothing to equal them in modern wars. They have lost nearly all of their horses, and most of them have been eaten

by the army. The soldiers were very glad to find dead horses,
those which had perhaps starved to death, that they might eat
them. The officers fared no better. I heard an officer say that he
had seen soldiers cut pieces out of live horses to eat, and without killing them."[11]

The exact date of the composition of the poem is not known;
but probably sometime in late November or early December of
1812, before beginning his carriage trip to death, Barlow wrote
the following bitter and powerful indictment of Napoleon and
his wars of conquest.

ADVICE TO A RAVEN IN RUSSIA

Black fool, why winter here? These frozen skies,
Worn by your wings and deafen'd by your cries,
Should warn you hence, where milder suns invite,
And day alternates with his mother night.
        You fear perhaps your food may fail you there—   5
Your human carnage, that delicious fare,
That lured you higher, following still your friend,
The great Napoleon to the world's bleak end.
You fear, because the southern climes pour'd forth
Their clustering nations to infest the north,   10
Bavarians, Austrians, those who drink the Po
And those who skirt the Tuscan seas below,
With all Germania, Neustria, Belgia, Gaul,
Doom'd here to wade thro slaughter to their fall,
You fear he left behind no wars, to feed   15
His feather'd cannibals and nurse the breed.
        Fear not, my screamer, call your greedy train,
Sweep over Europe, hurry back to Spain,
You'll find his legions there; the valiant crew
Please best their master when they toil for you.   20
Abundant there they spread the country o'er
And taint the breeze with every nation's gore,
Iberian, Lusian, British widely strown;
But still more wide and copious flows their own.
        Go where you will; Calabria, Malta, Greece,   25
Egypt and Syria still his fame increase,
Domingo's fatten'd isle and India's plains
Glow deep with purple drawn from Gallic veins.
No raven's wing can stretch the flight so far
As the torn bandrols of Napoleon's war.   30
Choose then your climate, fix your best abode,
He'll make you deserts and he'll bring you blood.

How could you fear a dearth? have not mankind,
Tho slain by millions, millions left behind?
Has not CONSCRIPTION still the power to wield   35
Her annual faulchion o'er the human field?
A faithful harvester! or if a man
Escape that gleaner, shall he scape the BAN?
The triple BAN, that like the hound of hell
Gripes with joles, to hold his victim well.   40
    Fear nothing then, hatch fast your ravenous brood,
Teach them to cry to Buonaparte for food;
They'll be like you, of all his suppliant train,
The only class that never cries in vain.
For see what natural benefits you lend!   45
(The surest way to fix the mutual friend)
While on his slaughter'd troops are fed,
You cleanse his camp and carry off his dead.
Imperial scavenger! but now you know,
Your work is vain amid these hills of snow.   50
His tentless troops are marbled through with frost
And change to crystal when the breath is lost.
Mere trunks of ice, tho limb'd like human frames,
And lately warm'd with life's endearing flames.
They cannot taint the air, the world impest.   55
Nor can they tear one fiber from their breast.
No! from their visual sockets as they lie,
With beak and claw you cannot pluck an eye,
The frozen orb, preserving still its form,
Defies your talons as it braves the storm,   60
But stands and stares to God, as if to know
In what curst hands he leaves his world below.
    Fly then, or starve; tho all the dreadful road
From Minsk to Moskow with their bodies strow'd
May count some Myriads, yet they can't suffice   65
To feed you more beneath these dreary skies.
Go back and winter in the wilds of Spain;
Feast there awhile, and in the next campaign
Rejoin your master; for you'll find him then,
With his new million of the race of men,   70
Clothed in his thunders, all his flags unfurl'd,
Raging and storming o'er the prostrate world!
    War after war his hungry soul requires,
State after state shall sink beneath his fires,
Yet other Spains in victim smoke shall rise   75
And other Moskows suffocate the skies,
Each land lie reeking with its peoples slain
And not a stream run bloodless to the main.

Till men resume their souls, and dare to shed
Earth's total vengeance on the monster's head,   80
Hurl from his blood-built throne this king of woes,
Dash him to dust, and let the world repose.[12]

All of Barlow's hopes for mankind were frozen in the Russian waste land. Much of the poem's bitterness is produced by the heavy irony which Barlow employs. He asks the raven why he is in Russia where the corpses are so frozen that they are inedible, and he assures the raven that Napoleon will provide food— "that delicious fare"—throughout Europe, including the warmer climates of Spain. The good that Napoleon does for the raven is turned, of course, into evidence of Napoleon's madness and of the general state of a civilization that would allow this madness.

Barlow makes his point emphatically in the strongest and most effective image he ever created. Lines 51–62 describe the frozen corpses which covered the Russian landscape. The emphasis is on the complete immobility and dehumanization of the frozen figures, which are "marbled through with frost" and which even the raven cannot tear apart. The final irony is of the eyes, frozen forever open, staring at God for answers which they are incapable of seeing and, perhaps, which are not even there to be seen. The irony within the poem is quite evident, but the irony of the poem, when placed within the context of Barlow's other writings becomes even stronger, especially when one realizes that this statement is Barlow's final one about mankind.

The basic motivation behind most of Barlow's prose was to give advice which would help mankind to progress toward some perfect or near perfect state, the vision of which was the central image of most of his poetry. In "Advice to a Raven in Russia," Barlow combined these two ideas and presented both in almost totally opposite ways. His advice is not to mankind but to an "Imperial scavenger" for the final destruction of mankind. His vision is not the final one of the earthly millennium with which he ended most of his poems, but rather of "war after war" as Napoleon continued to sweep back and forth across Europe. Previously, Barlow had grown ecstatic when considering the future state of society; now, all he could suggest was a vague overthrow of Napoleon and a world at least in repose. Barlow's concept of progress, which gradually evolved from a self-per-petuating, almost automatic process to one in which mankind controlled its own movement, suddenly came to a complete halt in the frozen winter of northern Europe. Immobility—the frozen fixedness of Dante's final circle—was the final description left by Barlow, the poet of progress.

"Advice to a Raven in Russia" appears to represent the end of an optimist. It would be foolish, however, to overdramatize the apparently complete reversal in Barlow's thinking. Had he lived through Napoleon's retreat and returned to America, a life-time of faith in man would probably have reasserted itself. Bar-low had been discouraged before: he had been betrayed by partners in an early business venture; he had been disillusioned with the course of the French Revolution; he had been severely attacked by former friends and denounced as an anarchist and as an atheist. These setbacks he had overcome, and it is im-probable that he would not have felt differently about the state of the world when he was once more back at "Kalorama." The fact remains, however, that he did not return and that "Advice to a Raven in Russia" is the final word we have from his pen.

Leon Howard summed up the reputation of Barlow's poetry as follows: "The man who had remained in Europe in order to help renovate mankind succeeded merely in becoming the poet of cornmeal mush, and to most students of American literature he is little more than that at the present day."[13] But he deserves a little better. When he was least self-conscious about his poetry, he produced lines which rank high in an essentially unpoetic age.

CHAPTER *5*

The Vision of Joel Barlow

IN AN AGE OF poor poetry, most of Barlow's was mediocre; in an age of great prose, Barlow's was among the best. Only in prose did Barlow consistently practice that moderation and rationality that he called for in everything he wrote. Although the best prose of the national period is noted for the logic of its argument and balance of its construction as men discussed and debated the course their country should take in domestic and foreign policy, much of it consisted of bitter name-calling tirades against persons with different political and religious ideas. Although Barlow was constantly attacked by his political enemies as an anarchist, an atheist, and a traitor, it must be said to his credit that rarely did he write against a particular individual, and then he emphasized the ideas the man held rather than his personality or his private affairs.

Throughout all of Barlow's prose one finds a number of ideas that reveal his unified and consistent view of man, of society, and of the role given to government. Barlow was always giving advice to anyone who would listen, partly because he thought he had something important to say and partly because he had a firm faith in the ability of people to respond correctly when they understood the choice they have. At the basis of all his advice is a belief that America had almost miraculously discovered a unique combination of political concepts that would produce greatness on the North American continent and spread inevitably throughout the Western world. The republican principles adopted by the framers of the Constitution insure liberty to all citizens, and the federation of the states insures security for the nation. Other countries had utilized one concept or the other, but only the United States had combined them.

Two of Barlow's other recurring themes describe courses of action necessary to insure both a republican and a federalized country. First, all men need to be educated so that they can determine wisely how their republic shall be run; they are the rulers, and they must understand the choices confronting them. Second, the citizens of the country must develop a feeling that they are part of one total political and social unit and not isolated from the main portion of the nation. To insure this unity, transportation must be facilitated throughout the country; waterways, bridges, and roads must be constructed and maintained. In short, attention must be given to internal improvements which will become even more vital as the country expands westward and northward, an expansion which Barlow believed was inevitable.

In order to obtain the funds necessary for these projects which would insure a federalized democracy, Barlow urged continually that the United States reduce and finally eliminate its national debt by instituting economic pressures for a standing army and a large navy and by discontinuing the practice of funding. Barlow also believed that the country could prosper by insisting on complete freedom of the seas, thereby increasing greatly its own commerce and, again, reducing the need for a large navy. Practices such as these would, he thought, provide more than enough funds for the internal-improvement projects he suggested.

Finally, the humanitarian strain in all of Barlow's thinking, his deep concern for the results of both the French and the American revolutions, and his belief in the sovereignty of the individual within the limits of social responsibility produced two themes again manifest in most of his prose. One of the sources of greatest sorrow for Barlow during his last twenty-five years was the almost constant friction between his native and his adopted countries. He believed that if the two could understand each other, they could lead Europe into a republic resembling that established in North America. Consequently, he spent a great deal of effort trying to persuade America that France was her friend; and he suffered many personal attacks in the effort. But, perhaps the most serious attacks came as a result of his religious beliefs. Because of his support of the "atheistic" French and because of his comments on established religion in both his poetry and his prose, he was regarded by the proper

New Englanders as a lost soul. Occasionally, Barlow paused to point out that the basis for his religious belief had broadened but not crumbled and that a toleration of religious views would be desirable; but, generally, his prose was concerned almost completely with political issues.

Beginning with a firm belief in the importance of the individual and the individual nation, Barlow advised several governments and two generations in several specific courses of action. An examination of his prose reveals a deeply concerned and consistently logical humanitarian as well as a skilled writer.

I   Advice to the Privileged Orders

Barlow's best-known, most highly praised prose work is *Advice to the Privileged Orders.* One of the many replies to Edmund Burke's *Reflections on the Revolution in France*, Barlow's has always remained in the shadow of Thomas Paine's *The Rights of Man*, although at least one student of Barlow insists that, "as literature, it far surpasses *The Rights of Man.*"[1] *Advice to the Privileged Orders* was published in February, 1792, at a time when Barlow's faith in the French Revolution was at its highest. He was convinced that the revolution would sweep western Europe, crushing all forms of authoritarianism before it; and his advice to the privileged orders was that they should recognize the inevitability of this movement for their own good. At the conclusion of the Introduction, he states his purpose: "Taking it for granted, therefore, that a general revolution is at hand, whose progress is irresistible, my object is to contemplate its probable effects, and to comfort those who are afflicted at the prospect" (107).

Behind all Barlow's thinking are two basic principles: *"all men are equal in rights,* and . . . the *government is their own"* (120). He believed that governments had traditionally worked against these two ideas; some men were given rights others did not have, and the mass always worked solely for the small minority who had these privileges. Barlow felt strongly that these false notions were vestiges of feudal society and that they could be changed by appealing to the reasoning power of the people. When they understood, these remnants of feudalism would be eliminated as they had been for the most part in America and in France. Barlow then proposed to examine eight different areas of society to show how each has developed from the feudal notion of inequality and from its political extension, monarchy. The areas he intended to examine in successive chapters were the feudal system; the church; the military; the administration of justice; revenue and public expenditure; the means of subsistence; literature, sciences, and arts; and war and peace. The work was never completed, however; only the first five chapters were published.

Barlow saw the basic evil of feudalism as the continued dominance of the few over the many, and the function of all areas of the feudal society was to maintain these unnatural distinctions. In society, such practices as primogeniture and entailment contribute to this distinction by perpetuating territorial rights based on heredity rather than on merit. But Barlow reserves most of his attack for the institutions of the church and the military which he believes are directly responsible for the perpetuation of the privileged orders. In Chapter Two, Barlow made a distinction between religion and a state church which, in his thinking, have nothing to do with each other. He states his idea in his usual direct and emphatic language: *"The existence of any kind of liberty is incompatible with the existence of any kind of church"* (135). Religious leaders, when made an agent of the state, resort to superstition and threat of damnation to maintain the status quo. Furthermore, history has shown that men become even more ferocious as they believe they are doing God's will, or as Barlow succinctly put it: *"Nations are cruel in proportion as they are guided by priests"* (139).

Another instrument of the government which Barlow believed was retained solely because it kept the masses in subjugation was the military. His reasons and the relationship between the state church and the military can be seen in the following quotation:

Honor, like religion, is an original, indelible sentiment of the mind, an indispensable ingredient in our nature. But its object is incapable of precise definition; and consequently, though given us in aid of the more definable feelings of morality, it is capable of total perversion, of losing sight of its own original nature, and still retaining its name; of pursuing the destruction of moral sentiments, instead of being their ornament; of debasing, instead of supporting, the dignity of man. . . . (147)

Indeed, I can see but one reason in nature, why the principle of honor should be selected from all human incentives, and relied on for the support of the military system; it is because it was *convenient for the governing power.* . . . (148-49)

Barlow's primary objection to the military systems of Europe is that they distort the natural relationship among men by placing some individuals above most and because they sustain this distinction by appealing to the vague concept of honor, just as the priests appeal to the equally vague concept of religion. Feudal society kept the military leadership in the hands of the nobility, thereby increasing class distinctions. Barlow's solution was to establish a militia of citizen soldiers, advice which he was to pass on to his native country several years later.

Chapters Four and Five continue Barlow's revelations of sources of inequality in society, but here Barlow also begins to emphasize his second point—the responsibility that the government has for the individual. Chapter Four, "The Administration of Justice," discusses theories of justice and penology. First, he believed that no government has the right to punish an individual until it has fully instructed him in the consequences of his action. Since each individual, except those who are incompetent due to natural defects, is capable of determining what is best for himself, it follows that proper instruction could eliminate almost completely the need for punishment. The faith is in man, but the responsibility is given to society. The court systems of European countries, and especially of England, are so involved and weighted down with feudal trappings that the individual simply cannot find his way through the legal maze. Barlow proposes that the courts should be understandable and inexpensive (bribery increases the expense), as well as easily accessible to the people. Pointing with pride to America, Barlow insists that these reforms are possible.

Turning to "Revenue and Expenditure" in Chapter Five, Barlow once again finds the origin of today's evils in feudal organization. Originally, the vassals received land in return for a certain amount of military service, a practice which evolved into an exchange of land for cultivating a certain area, and, finally, the transformation of labor to fixed monetary sums in exchange for protection. Barlow does not oppose taxation, however, so much as hidden or indirect taxation, because this deprives the individual of a choice and is too easily subject to the desires of the monarchy, church, or both. Unjust application of taxes always results in a large public debt, high salaries, undue attachment of salaries, and other abuses which only tend to perpetuate an unnatural and unfair distinction among people. Barlow's *Advice to the Privileged Orders* is a response to Burke's contention that societal change is unwise because it disturbs the status quo. Disturbance, Barlow maintained, is just what the status quo needs and will receive. The people, if only made knowledgeable, will demand equality and a government which will serve them. In "The Conspiracy of Kings" Barlow took a dull hatchet and chopped away at Burke and the monarchists. In this work, he cut with surgeonlike deftness into the heart of society and suggested a cure.

In his poetry Barlow felt a need to use a style which seems overly conventionalized and too contrived to a later age. His prose, however, remains just as vital and effective today as it was when it was written. *Advice to the Privileged Orders* is effective primarily because of Barlow's use of rationality and the logical progression of his thought. His faith in the reasonable nature of man is seen vividly in the style he chose to adopt. For instance, the development of his argument for a militia, instead of a standing army, is presented step by step, beginning with the basic principle that all men are equal:

> Only admit the original, unalterable truth, that *all men are equal in their rights*, and the foundation of everything is laid; to build the superstructure requires no effort but that of natural deduction. The first necessary deduction will be, that the people will form an equal representative government; in which it will be impossible for *orders* or *privileges* to exist for a moment; and consequently the first materials for standing armies will be converted into peaceable members of the state. Another deduction follows, That the people will be universally armed: they will assume those weapons for security, which the art of war has invented for destruction. You will then have removed the *necessity* of a standing army by the organization of the legislature, and the *possibility* of it by the arrangement of the militia; for it is as impossible for an armed soldiery to exist in an armed nation, as for a nobility to exist under an equal government. (161–62)

The logical structure of his argument is additionally strengthened by the balance and parallelism of his sentences. At the end of Chapter One, Barlow describes France now that it has shed its feudal shackles:

> But in France their hands are at last untied; the charm is broken, and the feudal system, with all its infamous idolatries, has fallen to the ground. Honor is restored to the heart of man, instead of being suspended from his button-hole; and useful industry gives a title to respect. The men that were formerly dukes and marquisses are now exalted to farmers, manufacturers and merchants; the rising generation among all classes of people are forming their maxims on a just estimate of things; and society is extracting the poisoned dagger which conquest had planted in her vitals. (128)

Advice to the Privileged Orders reflects in content and in style a reasonable man speaking confidently to other reasonable men.

II   *Advice to the French and Italians*

The year 1792 saw two other important pamphlets published by Barlow, both of which are related to France's attempts to revise its 1791 constitution. In October, 1792, Barlow's friend, Thomas Paine, delivered before the National Convention Barlow's *A Letter to the National Convention of France On the Defects in the Constitution of 1791, and the extent of the amendments to be applied*, in which he reaffirmed his faith in republican principles and presented a list of thirteen suggestions for the new constitution. Near the end of that year Barlow wrote *A Letter Addressed to the People of Piedmont On the advantages of the French Revolution, and the necessity of adopting its principles in Italy*, an appeal to the people of Piedmont which bordered the French province of Savoy to welcome the French army which promised to liberate them in the spring. This pamphlet restated the principles of the French Revolution and its inevitable spread throughout Europe.

Speaking of *Letter to the National Convention*, Vernon Louis Parrington made the following observation: "Two ideas determined his thinking: the doctrine of the sovereignty of the majority will, and the doctrine of government as a social agent."[2] Barlow attempted in the first part of his letter to show "*that kings can do no good*," that a state church is evil, and that the people can best judge what is best for themselves. In the second part, he listed his thirteen proposals—specific suggestions which would insure the right of the majority to rule themselves.

After attacking a monarchy, even a limited one such as France still had, because of its expense and inevitable corruption and because the king, through flattery and the security of an inherited title, would probably be either weak or wicked, he asserts his faith in majority will: "A republic of beavers or of monkies, I believe, could not be benefited by receiving their laws from men, any more than men could be in being governed by them." (40) And more directly: "The sure and only characteristic of a good law is, *that it be the perfect expression of the will of the nation*" (41).

Barlow's thirteen proposals show how he could translate political and social theory into practical suggestions. It is impossible to determine how influential Barlow's advice was in the framing of the 1793 Constitution, although it did incorporate several of the ideas Barlow described. It is equally impossible to determine how much of an impact the United States Constitution had on Barlow's thinking.[3] It is certain, however, that *Letter to the National Convention* provides a link between these two republican statements. Barlow's proposals are as follows:

1. Because property requirement is a vestige of the monarchy, base representation solely on population.
2. Reduce the minimum age for a voter to twenty years, thus increasing the total number of voters.
3. Do not restrict citizenship by national boundaries. Give citizenship to all who settle in France and allow those who move to other countries to retain their citizenship.
4. Hold annual elections in order to keep representatives in touch with their constituents, and prohibit anyone from serving more than two years in every four in order to insure a larger number of active participants.
5. Keep salaries at a minimum so that no one would pursue an office for monetary reward or the possibility of graft.
6. Make certain that representatives represent the people of the regions that chose them and not the nation as a whole.
7. Eliminate imprisonment for debt.
8. Reform penal practices and abolish the death penalty.

9. Require the government to undertake public instruction. An informed electorate is necessary to a republic.

10. Eliminate public lotteries.

11. Reject colonies.

12. Eliminate the standing army because if it is weak, it will fail to defend the country, and if it is strong, it would be a threat to the liberty of the people. Develop instead a militia.

13. Make provisions for amendments.

A Letter Addressed to the People of Piedmont arose from Barlow's belief that the French Revolution would sweep Europe. Piedmont lay next to Savoy, separated by the Alps. During December, 1792, it was reasonable to assume that the French army would be in Italy by the spring of 1793; therefore, Barlow hoped to prevent bloodshed by convincing the Italians that the French were their friends and that they would be much better off under new rule. Once again, Barlow demonstrated his belief that a rational appeal to rational people is sufficient to spread truth. When speaking of the French Revolution as a movement to be emulated, he said: "If the example were bad, your good sense would teach you to shun it; it would need only to be known, to be despised, and it ought to be explained to all people, that they might learn to avoid such a dangerous innovation. If it be good, it ought to be taught by your teachers, and imitated by all the world. But be assured that the very caution they use to prevent your coming to the knowledge of the fact, is a proof that such a revolution would be an advantage to you and a disadvantage to them" (327).

His letter also gave him an opportunity to reply to some of the common accusations made against the revolution. In answer to the charge of atheism, he said that revolution had rid France of the state church, in this case Roman Catholicism, but that it also guaranteed freedom of worship to all religions. He answered the charge that private property was not allowed by saying that sinecures were paid for when seized and that church property always did belong to the people. Finally, he admitted that the charge of cruelty and murder was unfortunately true to some extent but that these actions were the result of habits instilled in the people by the former government.

After an implied ultimatum to the people of Piedmont to

join the revolution peacefully or have thousands slaughtered by the invincible French army, Barlow closed with a definition of France's role in the renovation of Europe. The forces of right and reason are combining to allow man to reconstruct society so that the masses instead of a few fortunate ones will benefit, and France is demonstrating that this reconstruction is not only possible but imminent:

> France has been forced into the field, to encounter this infamous combination of robbers, this war of all crimes against the principles of all virtue. She has undertaken the defense of human nature. She has assumed a new kind of tactique unknown to the art of war, and irresistible to the armies of kings. She has armed herself in the panoply of reason; her manifesto is the rights of man, her sword the pledge of peace. In this species of warfare we need not be astonished at her success. What people can resist the hand that comes to break their chains? The armies of liberty are every where triumphant, while their standards are scarcely stained with blood. Victory completes her work, before they arrive to celebrate the conquest; and the entrance of the French troops into the conquered country is regarded by the people rather as the procession of a civic feast than as the dreaded violence of war. Their general, instead of punishing the new recovered citizens with confiscation, imprisonment, and death, meets them in their Jacobine societies, and invites them to form their primary assemblies. The forts and garrisons which he erects to secure his conquests, are printing presses and reading clubs. (348–49)

Unfortunately for Barlow and the revolution, forces threatening France from without and violence from within made the spring invasion of Italy impractical. Barlow's words, however, remain a passionate defense of the principles of the French Revolution.

III   *Advice to the Americans*

As the century moved toward its close, Napoleon Bonaparte was solidifying his hold on a France that had largely departed from its earlier revolutionary ideals, a departure that Barlow found distressing but which did not prevent him from urging a closer bond between France and the United States. Furthermore, in America, it began to look as though the Republicans might break the Federalist grip on the presidency in 1800. These two developments now caused Joel Barlow, who had been giving advice to the rulers of Europe for nearly a decade, to turn his attention to the domestic and foreign policy of his native country; and, in a series of letters and pamphlets, he helped to heal the dangerous breach between his two countries.

The *Letters from Paris* were completed in Paris on March 4, 1799, and December 20, 1799, and were probably printed in 1800. The first letter, "On the System of Policy Hitherto Pursued by Their Government," was written in response to a letter which Barlow had sent to Washington and which was mangled by editors when it was published without his permission; the second letter, "On Certain Political Measures Proposed to Their Consideration," was concerned with Barlow's plan for a world society based on freedom of the seas. Barlow's advice to his fellow Americans was somewhat different from the advice he had been passing out in Europe earlier in the decade. Earlier he had seen France sowing peaceful revolutions throughout Europe; now he was urging the United States to avoid conflict, especially with France, and to work instead on the internal affairs of the country.

In both letters he suggested several ways in which the country could avoid a war which, after all, would divert funds needed elsewhere and simply increase the power of the federal government and in particular the executive branch. Barlow believed that the United States could avoid foreign entanglements by insisting on complete freedom of the seas for itself and for all nations. Since both public and private sources owed money to those countries who were plundering the seas, Barlow suggested a sequestering of these debts in proportion to the damage done to American shipping. This method, he felt, was an honorable and practical substitute for war. Barlow also believed that this principle of economic coercion could lead to a "United States of Europe." In fact, in the second letter, Barlow proposed a Maritime Convention made up of various countries which would insure freedom of the seas under penalty of a Ban of Commerce, consisting of prohibition of trade with the offending country and a penalty to be paid by that country. Cooperation of this sort could easily lead to more encompassing political cooperation.

Barlow opposed war, standing armies, and navies on moral

grounds; but he also opposed them because they were expensive, thereby draining off money needed elsewhere, and because they led to other questionable and equally expensive practices. One of these questionable practices which war necessitates is the funding system or the building up of a large public debt. In Chapter Five of *Advice to the Privileged Orders*, Barlow argued at length against passing one generation's debts on to later generations; and he is again saying the same thing. Furthermore, he believed that a national debt would bind the United States to nations that were inferior and, therefore, restrict the progress that a young, vigorous country should make. "Your physicians have gone to a decrepid [*sic*] intemperate old man, and borrowed his strong cordials, his bandages, and gouty velvet shoes, to administer them with cruel empiricism to a sturdy plowboy" (381).

In the second letter, Barlow's advice becomes most specific when he explains how America can insure freedom for the people within its borders. Barlow, as well as others, was concerned at this time with the future of those lands west and north of the United States; in fact, he expressed some concern for the Western states which he felt were being isolated from the government located in the East. The United States cannot rely upon European means of insuring unity, a state religion, or a threat from neighboring countries; therefore, it should develop its own means of insuring unity. As Barlow expressed elsewhere and was to express later, he believed that improved means of transportation and the construction of a national system of republican education—physical and mental contact—would insure a stable country. He urged that the national debt be eliminated as soon as possible so that this money could be used for the construction of a system of roads and canals "to harmonize the interests of the states, and to strengthen their present union" (436). And in his discussion of the need for education, he stated with his usual clarity the vital connection between education and a representative democracy:

A universal attention to the education of youth, and a republican direction given to the elementary articles of public instruction, are among the most essential means of preserving liberty in any country where it is once enjoyed; especially in the United States. The representative system must necessarily degenerate, and become an instrument of tyranny, rather than of liberty, where there is an extraordinary disparity of information between the generality of the citizens and those who aspire to be their chiefs. And as to the federal ties between the different states, how shall they be maintained but by extending the views and enlightening the minds of those whose votes are frequently to be consulted, and whose actions are always irresistible by their numbers, and the direction which they take. (436–37)

Within a year of writing these letters to his fellow citizens, the crisis with France had eased and Barlow's friend and political ally, Thomas Jefferson, was elected president. Those ideals which Barlow had argued for and suffered slander for now showed signs of being realized. The need for political debating declined, but Barlow could still come forth with advice when the occasion demanded.

IV   *A National University*

Although much of Barlow's literary efforts during the last twelve years of his life went into his revision of *The Vision of Columbus*, into the translation of Volney's *Ruins*, into work on his proposed history of the United States, and into other assorted projects, he did find time to gather together his thoughts on education and to propose in 1806 a "Prospectus of a National Institution," which he felt would insure freedom and promote republican principles in America. As in the second letter from Paris, he saw education as a means of uniting the country: "It is most essential to the happiness of the people and to the preservation of their republican principles, that this tendency to a separation should be overbalanced by superior motives to a harmony of sentiment" (483).

But, in his prospectus, Barlow goes beyond assigning a simple contributory role to education; here he makes specific suggestions for its organization and suggests an institution not unlike the universities which were to develop toward the end of the century. His aim was to combine two objects: "These are the advancement of knowledge by associations of scientific men, and the dissemination of its rudiments by the instruction of youth" (482), or, as he said more succinctly later on in the prospectus, by "research and instruction." Barlow also aimed at combining practical and theoretical research.

The scope of Barlow's project was grasped by Leon Howard: "It was a deliberately ambitious, forward-looking project, much more advanced than any of the proposals previously submitted by Benjamin Rush, James Sullivan, Samuel H. Smith, DuPont de Nemours, and others. Barlow thought that the world needed another Bacon, and, in a limited way, he was trying to outline a practical method for the advancement of learning in America."[4] Although Barlow made no suggestions that were completely original, he did enumerate fifteen different types of schools and projects which the French government supported and which might be found in a national institution. In actuality, of course, Barlow is suggesting these for consideration: (1) The School of Mines, (2) The School of Roads and Bridges, (3) The Conservatory of Arts (useful arts and trades), (4) The Museum of Natural History, (5) The Museum of Arts (fine arts), (6) The National Library, (7) The Mint, (8) The Military School, (9) The Prytaneum (School of general, military, and nautical science for fatherless boys), (10) The College of France, (11) The School of Medicine, (12) The Veterinary School, (13) The Observatory, (14) Bureau of Longitude (nautical and geographical exploration and discoveries), and (15) Polytechnic School (similar to the modern graduate school.[5]

In addition to these projects, Barlow thought the Institution might sponsor a series of free lectures, reading rooms, and laboratories such as those sponsored by the French Lyceum of Arts or the English Royal Institution; and it could also provide a relief fund for indigent authors and their families comparable to the British Literary Fund. As is obvious, Barlow had in mind something going beyond even today's large university; for he desired a central agency which would oversee the propagation and distribution of knowledge. Although he suggested that the institution have its headquarters and several departments in Washington, he foresaw many of its schools scattered throughout the country. "In short," he said, "no rudiment of knowledge should be below its attention, no height of improvement above its ambition, no corner of our empire beyond its vigilant activity for collecting and diffusing information" (515).

Barlow realized that the federal government was unable to finance a project as wieldy as this one, however deserving it might be. Nevertheless, he did believe that a start might be made; and, in an appendix to his Prospectus, he suggested that private donations might allow plans to begin immediately. All in all, "Prospectus of a National Institution" is Barlow's attempt to insure those republican principles for which he fought and argued throughout most of his adult life. His earliest prose revealed a faith in man's ability to choose what is best for himself if he has all the information. Now Barlow hoped to construct a mammoth edifice which would insure that each citizen has that information. As Jefferson and others well knew, the continuation of a successful representative democracy depended upon an enlightened electorate. The theme of education runs throughout everything Barlow wrote, for his belief in its necessity was as strong as his belief in America's future.

V   *The Later Years*

These complementary ideas of education and America's destiny were eloquently combined in prose at least one more time before Barlow left in pursuit of Napoleon. In 1807, Joel Barlow delivered a July 4 oration which rose above the usual descriptions of events of the war and catalogues of national heroes; instead, it presented a restatement of America's unique position, a reference to its future glories, and an insistence that these glories could be achieved only if Americans worked consciously toward them. As in his *Letters from Paris* eight years earlier, Barlow maintained that a sprawling country could be unified only if its transportation facilities were improved and its public instruction increased. The address itself seems a bit disjointed, ending as it does with a sudden reference to Fulton's submarine as the answer to naval tyranny; however, Barlow does reach eloquent heights and convincing logic when he calls for the education of all citizens:

In a monarchy the education of the prince is justly deemed a concern of the nation. It is done at their expense; and why is it so? it is because they are deeply interested in his being well educated; that he may be able to administer the government well, to conduct the concerns of the nation wisely, on their own constitutional principles. My friends, is it not even more important that our princes, our millions of princes, should be educated for their station, than the single prince of a monarchy? If a single prince goes wrong, obstinately and incurably wrong, he may be set aside for another, without overturning the state. But if our sovereigns in their multitudinous exercise of power should become obstinate and incurable in wrong, you cannot set them aside. But they will set you aside; they will set themselves aside; they will crush the state and convulse the nation. The result is military despotism, dismemberment of the great republic, and, after a sufficient course of devastation by civil wars, the settlement of a few ferocious monarchies, prepared to act over again the same degrading scenes of mutual encroachment and vindictive war, which disgrace modern Europe; and from which many writers have told us, that mankind are never to be free. (531)

The progress of Barlow's thinking from his days as a Connecticut Wit to those as consultant to the president may be seen by comparing this address with another made twenty years earlier on the same occasion at a meeting of the Connecticut Society of the Cincinnati. "An Oration, Delivered at the North Church in Hartford" also praised the work of the Revolution and vaguely predicted future glories for America. The oration also contained a statement of faith in the ability of the majority to choose wisely and in the power of reasonable discourse. Missing in this oration is Barlow's later discovery that man must carve out his own destiny; hence, his concern for bridges, canals, and schools. In place of these practical suggestions, Barlow of 1787 resorted to flights of rhetoric without content:

Without an efficient government our Independence will cease to be a blessing. Shall that glow of patriotism and unshaken perseverence, which have been so long conspicuous in the American character, desert us at our utmost need? Shall we lose sight of our own happiness, because it has grown familiar by a near approach? Shall thy labours, O Washington, be bestowed in vain? Hast thou conducted us to independence and peace, and shall we not receive the blessings at thy hands? Where are the shades of our fallen friends? and what is their language on this occasion? *Warren, Montgomery, Mercer, Wooster, Scammel* and *Laurens*, all ye hosts of departed heroes! rich is the treasure you have lavished in the cause, and prevalent the price you have paid for our freedom. Shall the purchase be neglected? the fair inheritance lie without improvement, exposed to every daring invader? Forbid it, honour, forbid it, gratitude; and oh, may Heaven avert the impending evil. (8-9)

Fortunately, Barlow replaced this school-room display in his later prose with the direct, forceful, reasonable style of his maturity.

Barlow, of course, published a number of attacks, replies, and rebuttals in the press of his day, many, doubtless, unidentifiable. The Republican-Federalist pamphlet warfare was constant and often vicious. Of Barlow's contributions, however, only two were published separately, one for political reasons and the other for religious. The political pamphlet was published in 1811, shortly before Barlow departed for Europe, and it was written at the request of the Madison administration. Madison's secretary of state, Robert Smith, was dismissed for ineptness and for his unwillingness to carry out the foreign policy of the administration. In retaliation, he produced a personal attack on the president and revealed information which should have remained confidential. "Review of Robert Smith's Address" did not descend to the level of Smith's attack, although it was political hackwork without the general statements of principle which characterize Barlow's better prose. Step by step he refutes Smith's accusations by pointing out in a crude satiric tone the folly of his thinking: he simply says something is wonderful when he means just the opposite. Although "Review of Robert Smith's Address" does no credit to Barlow as a statesman, it does demonstrate his reluctance to descend to name-calling when the occasion might warrant.

One of the most effective weapons used against Barlow throughout his mature life was the charge of atheism. In New England, the French Revolution itself was synonymous with atheism, and Barlow was thought to have been thoroughly corrupted by his extended stay in Europe. It is true, of course, that Barlow had rejected almost completely the Protestantism of his youth, many times expressing dissatisfaction with established religion because of its basically nonrational approach and because it could be used to support monarchies. Although Barlow nowhere delineated his religious convictions, it is possible to see in both his poetry and prose a liberal position developing which is not unlike that held by the Deists—in spite of Barlow's public declarations that he was not a Deist. Ironically, one of the most potentially destructive religious attacks on Barlow came not from his Federalist opponents but from one of his fellow revolutionaries in France. Henri Gregoire, former bishop of Blois and president of the National Convention, published a letter which he had sent to Barlow after examining *The Columbiad.* While expressing praise for its poetry, he, nevertheless, expressed regret at the antichristian implications of the poem and, specifically, at an engraving, *Final Destruction of Prejudices,* which depicted the cross as one of the prejudices which would be destroyed. In the course of his restrained attack on Barlow's poem, he noted that many of the injustices of the French Revolution had occurred after it renounced religion; and he predicted that the United States would become another Algiers if it took the same course.

This attack put Barlow in an extremely delicate position. He had to satisfy his old friend, Gregoire, and, by extension, all those possible readers of *The Columbiad* who might agree with him; but he also had to remain true to his own convictions. As Leon Howard points out, Barlow did not quite accomplish this reconciliation.[6] "Letter to Henry Gregoire" is an excellent example of Barlow's reasonableness and tact; however, his assertions about his religious position are, at best, misleading. In spite of the fact that the engraving was completed and finished for publication in England before Barlow ever saw it, he accepted responsibility for it and attempted to justify its offensive symbolism. First, he made a distinction between the Puritan abhorrence of idols and the Catholic reliance upon objects. He believed that Gregoire was confusing the symbol with the idea it represents—a fault Barlow finds in all religions. Furthermore, he claimed that his work is moral and even Christian because it supports and encourages all those principles which are moral and Christian. On this statement, he based his assertion that he had always been a Christian. The argument revolves around a semantic discussion of the word "Christian," and Barlow must have known he was playing with terms in order to satisfy both his friends and his enemies.

To Gregoire's accusation that the French revolutionary extremists were atheistic, Barlow replied that he was never an extremist; furthermore, he insisted that he had never renounced his religion publicly before the National Assembly as some of his enemies tried to prove. Although Gregoire had not suggested that Barlow had done these things. Gregoire nevertheless published a second letter saying unequivocally that these accusations were false. The over-all result of this exchange was a more favorable depiction of Barlow's religion. Once again Barlow accomplished his goal through reason and through consideration for his fellow man.

Joel Barlow's great period of prose was the last decade of the eighteenth century. In a series of public documents he propounded a political and social theory together with practical suggestions for its implementation. His advice, though not original, is important because it so clearly and forcefully presents a view of man and society that is both consistent and visionary. As in his poetry, Barlow saw in his prose the possibility of a better, even a perfect, world; but, unlike his poetry, which gives generalized glimpses of this future utopia, his prose explains carefully how this utopia might be realized in the near future. This prose presentation and not *The Columbiad* was his greatest gift to America.

CHAPTER 6

The Largeness of the Man

BARLOW'S REPUTATION rests primarily on his poetry, a poetry which reveals an imitative, grandiose proclaimer of America's future. In many ways, however, the faults of Barlow's poetry are those of his unpoetic age; as a result, his poetry produces a false and misleading portrait of the man. The broad cosmopolitanism of his personal life and the political and social thinking of his maturity never penetrated the more narrow realm of his poetics. He, as did every poet writing then, called for self-reliance while relying upon the borrowed lines of the English Augustans; and he did produce, in spite of his many other activities, an impressive amount of poetry. *The Columbiad* overwhelms by sheer weight alone.

Unfortunately, however, as Leon Howard has pointed out, the poets of this era, including Joel Barlow, often confused quantity with quality;[1] and, what proved even more detrimental to their poetry, they often confused patriotic sentiment with poetic merit. It is possible to place Barlow's poetry within the tradition of American verse and to see some value in its relationship to later poetry, and Roy Harvey Pearce has done so with *The Columbiad*, revealing its place in the development of the American epic through Whitman's *Leaves of Grass* and Williams' *Paterson*.[2] But such a study says nothing of the intrinsic value of the poetry. The fact remains that, except for a few lines from *The Vision of Columbus*, parts of "The Hasty Pudding," and certain images from "To a Raven in Russia," Barlow produced no poetry of lasting poetic value. Simultaneously, however, one must remember that these exceptions are among the best that were produced in the early national period.

The difference in quality between Barlow's poetry and his prose can be easily seen by examining one of his favorite ideas which has been presented in both prose and poetry. In documents such as his *Letters from Paris* and his July 4 *Oration*

Delivered at Washington, Barlow stressed, as has been discussed, the importance of internal developments as a means of insuring the unity of the country: roads, canals, and bridges would keep the people in contact with each other. When this same idea was expressed in poetry, the result was one of Barlow's worst poems, "On the Discoveries of Captain Lewis." Enraptured by the thought of Lewis and Clarke opening up new passages to the west, he penned his tribute, two stanzas of which follow:

> These four brother floods [rivers], like a garland of flowers,
> Shall entwine all our states in a band,
> Conform and confederate their wide-spreading powers,
> And their wealth and their wisdom expand.
>
> From Darien to Davis one garden shall bloom,
> Where war's wearied banners are furl'd;
> And the far-scenting breezes that waft its perfumes,
> Shall settle the storms of the world.[3]

The close reasoning of his prose is replaced by an exaggeration that almost becomes inanity.

Another weakness in Barlow's poetry was caught by Gordon Bigelow who observed that American poets of this period were too self-consciously aware of playing out their role on the world's stage, that they "wrote by rule only": "Their poems were usually artifacts, sometimes constructed with great ingenuity, but more often loosely pasted together from unknown elements. Only rarely were they, like the poems of Milton, new and original products, created by a refusion of these elements. American poems of this period are often 'mere' rhetoric in the sense that they are mere stylistic, lacking the illumination which can come from a radiant inner core of poetic imagination and emotion."[4]

The best prose of the period, including Barlow's, almost completely reverses this condition. Rhetorical devices, such as balance and antithesis, were used effectively to underscore the appeal to reason that was the basis of the thought being expressed. An important bond existed between form and content that was almost entirely missing in the poetry, and the result is that Barlow's prose still speaks cogently to the world while most of his poetry is as dated as powdered wigs.

All commentators on Barlow's life and works arrive at the

point when they must confess that Barlow was greater than his literary output and perhaps should be remembered primarily for what he contributed as a citizen of the world. Indeed, his biographer, James Woodress, sees him as an archetype of the American character: "We can also see this able man who never quite achieved real greatness as the progenitor of us all. As poet trying to articulate America's future importance, as cosmopolite trying to place his country in the world community, as enlightened defender of democracy, as promoter of cultural enterprises, and as businessman, Barlow mirrors most of the impulses and experiences that make up the United States.[5]

Leon Howard regards him as a harbinger of modern America: "The peculiar value of his literary work as a whole lies in the fact that as a poet, describing visions his associates among the politicians had to conceal lest they be called fools, he revealed so many springs of action which, through the successes of more practical men, formed the institutions and affirmations that are among our most precious heritages from the eighteenth century. . . ."[6] And Vernon Louis Parrington simply emphasizes his humanity: "If he was not a great man, he was at least capable, open-minded, with a sensitive social conscience—certainly the most interesting and original of the Connecticut Wits. . . ."[7]

Statesman, pamphleteer, presidential consultant, businessman, revolutionary, and pretender to the title of Epic Poet of America, Barlow impresses one most with his humanitarianism, with his honest and constant concern for his fellow man. The largeness of the man is obscured by his epic pretentions, but it radiates from his best prose—and it is perhaps best seen in the many letters he wrote during his lifetime. It would be a mistake to overlook his correspondence in any examination of the man because in both his public and private letters can be seen the clarity and forcefulness of his style and the magnanimity of his spirit which typify his best writing. Two very dissimilar letters illustrate the depth and humanity of Joel Barlow.

In 1809, James Cheetham, editor of *American Citizen*, was busy writing his biography of Thomas Paine and was searching for bits of scandal which he could include. To this end, he sent a letter to Barlow requesting details of Paine's drunkenness and of his activities during the French Revolution. Barlow, realizing that Cheetham intended to emphasize Paine's questionable personal behavior, urged Cheetham to present Paine's character fairly or wait until later to publish his biography. Barlow knew he was taking an unpopular stand by supporting Paine; and he also knew that, despite protests, Cheetham would make the letter available to the public. The first half of the letter follows:

> I have received your letter calling for information relative to the life of Thomas Paine. It appears to me that this is not the moment to publish the life of that man in this country. His own writings are his best life, and these are not read at present.
>
> The greater part of readers in the United States will not be persuaded as long as their present feelings last, to consider him in any other light than as a drunkard and a deist. The writer of his life who should dwell on these topics, to the exclusion of the great and estimable traits of his real character, might indeed please the rabble of the age, who do not know him; the book might sell, but it would only tend to render the truth more obscure for the future biographer than it was before.
>
> But if the present writer should give us Thomas Paine *complete*, in all his character, as one of the most benevolent and disinterested of mankind, endowed with the clearest perception, an uncommon share of original genius, and the greatest breadth of thought; if this piece of biography should analyze his literary labors and rank him, as he ought to be ranked, among the brightest and most undeviating luminaries of the age in which he has lived, yet with a mind assailable by flattery, and receiving through that weak side a tincture of vanity which he was too proud to conceal; with a mind, though strong enough to bear him up and to rise elastic under the heaviest hand of oppression, yet unable to endure the contempt of his former friends and fellow-laborers, the rulers of the country that had received his first and greatest services; a mind incapable of looking down with serene compassion, as it ought, on the rude scoffs of their imitators, a new generation that knows him not; a mind that shrinks from their society, and unhappily seeks refuge in low company, or looks for consolation in the sordid, solitary bottle, till it sinks at last so far below its native elevation as to lose all respect for itself and to forfeit that of his best friends, disposing these friends almost to join with his enemies, and wish, though from different motives, that he would hasten to hide himself in the grave—if you are disposed and prepared to write his life *thus entire*, to fill up the picture to which these hasty strokes of outline give but a rude sketch with great vacuities, your book may be a useful one for another age, but it will not be relished, nor scarcely tolerated in this.[8]

This letter is the product of a public figure and participant in history who realizes how completely the people determine a man's reputation and how later generations will interpret and evaluate that reputation. The second letter is the product of a man not guided by a sense of history but by love and concern for his wife. It is a letter intended not for the public—indeed, hopefully, not even for Ruth. While in Algiers in 1796, Barlow had exposed himself to the plague by helping those who had already been afflicted, and he fully expected to contract the disease. During this time he wrote a letter to Ruth which was to be delivered only if he were to die. The letter reads in part:

My Dearest life & only love,
   I run no risque of alarming your extreme sensibility by writing this letter; since it is not my intention that it shall come into your hand unless & untill [sic] by some other channel you shall have been informed of the event which it anticipates as possible. For our happy union to be dissolved by death is indeed at every moment possible, but at this time there is an uncommon degree of danger that you may lose a life which I know you value more than you do your own. I say I *know* this, because I have long been taught, from our perfect sympathy of affection, to judge your heart by mine; and I can say solemnly & truely, [sic] as far as I know myself, that I have no other value for my own life than as a means of continuing a conjugal union with the best of women, the wife of my soul, my first, my last, my only love.[9]

Joel Barlow lived through this incredible period in Algiers; but, fourteen years later, he died under similar conditions— serving his country and separated from his wife. The American residents living in Paris at the time had a meeting at which they composed a letter of condolence and had it delivered to Mrs. Barlow. Her reply was simple and moving.

GENTLEMEN: —With sentiments of grateful acknowledgment I receive the assurances of esteem and regard which my resident countrymen in Paris bore my dear departed husband. He left his peaceful retreat with no other motive than a desire to be useful to his country. To that ardent desire he sacrificed his life, and devoted me to unceasing sorrow. Yet it will be most soothing to my afflicted heart to know that my countrymen do him justice, and will permit his memory to live in their remembrance.
                                        RUTH BARLOW[10]

Ruth's letter reflects Joel Barlow's humanity; his poetry reveals his hopes for America, and his prose demonstrates forcefully his proposals for realizing his vision. Joel Barlow played a minor but important role in the shaping of American history and literature.

Notes and References

Chapter One

1. Much of the biographical information in this chapter can be found also in James Woodress, *A Yankee's Odyssey: The Life of Joel Barlow* (Philadelphia, 1958), hereafter cited as Woodress; Theodore Zunder, *The Early Life of Joel Barlow* (New Haven, 1934), hereafter cited as Zunder; and Charles B. Todd, *Life and Letters of Joel Barlow* (New York, 1886), hereafter cited as Todd. Barlow's works were published in a facsimile edition by William K. Bottorff and Arthur L. Ford (ed.), *The Works of Joel Barlow*, 2 vols. (Gainesville, 1970), hereafter cited as *Works*. Page numbers within parentheses following quotations are to this edition. The prose is in Volume I, and the poetry is in Volume II.

2. Leon Howard, *The Connecticut Wits* (Chicago, 1943), p. 5. Hereafter cited as Howard.

3. Woodress, p. 34.

4. Howard, pp. 26–27.

5. Zunder, p. 66.

6. *Ibid.*, p. 73.

7. *Ibid.*, p. 44.

8. Woodress, pp. 44–45.

9. Zunder, p. 59.

10. Zunder, p. 113.

11. *Ibid.*, p. 114.

12. Woodress, p. 69.

13. Luther G. Riggs, ed., *The Anarchiad: A New England Poem* (New Haven, 1861), p. viii. A facsimile edition has been published by William K. Bottorff (Gainesville, 1967).

14. The whole range of literary nationalism in America has been treated by Benjamin Spencer, *The Quest for Nationality* (Syracuse, 1957).

15. Howard, p. 407.

16. Zunder, p. 206.

17. *Ibid.*, p. 203.

18. Howard, p. 159.
19. Woodress, pp. 85–86.
20. Zunder, pp. 224–25.
21. *Ibid.*, p. 230.
22. David B. Davis, ed., *Advice to the Privileged Orders* (Ithaca, 1956).
23. Woodress, p. 119.
24. *Ibid.*, p. 135.
25. Todd, p. 139.
26. Woodress, p. 198.
27. *Ibid.*, p. 197.
28. *Ibid.*, p. 241.
29. *Ibid.*, p. 249.
30. Todd, p. 220.
31. *Ibid.*, p. 233.
32. Howard, p. 332.
33. *Ibid.*, p. 336.
34. Woodress, p. 339.

Chapter Two

1. Zunder, p. 84.
2. The plan appears in its entirety in Todd, pp. 15–17, with several minor errors in transcription.
3. Zunder points out a further parallel between the first three books of *The Vision of Columbus* and several chapters from William Robertson's *The History of America*, pp. 86–87.
4. Actually, as Barlow points out, the imprisonment took place earlier, but, for dramatic purposes, it is placed here.
5. *The Vision of Columbus*, 5th ed. (Paris, 1793), p. 542.
6. Leon Howard, "The Late Eighteenth Century: An Age of Contradictions," in *Transitions in American Literary History*, ed. Harry Hayden Clark (Durham, 1954), p. 71.
7. Howard, p. 157.
8. *Ibid.*, p. 151.
9. Spencer, p. 14.
10. *Ibid.*, p. 67.
11. Howard, pp. 145–46.
12. *Ibid.*, pp. 146–49.
13. Quoted from an article in the *Catalogue of the American Art Association* (March 11–12, 1936), [n.p.]. A clipping of the article is in the New York Public Library.
14. Woodress, p. 86.
15. *Ibid.*, p. 87

Chapter Three

1. Howard, p. 309.

2. Since the fifth edition of *The Vision of Columbus* contains line numberings, all references to this edition are to book and lines and are enclosed in parentheses following the quotation. This edition is not included in *Works*.

3. Howard, p. 313.

4. All references to *The Columbiad* are to the 1825 edition containing "the last corrections of the author." It is this edition which is included in *Works*; hence, page numbers are to this edition. Barlow's "corrections" are minimal.

5. The poetry of the best of these Puritan poets, of course, transcended these limitations. Edward Taylor and Anne Bradstreet, for instance, produced genuine poetry that negates the distinction between form and content. One must remember, however, that both these poets had misgivings about having their poetry published. Also one need only recall the immense popularity of Michael Wigglesworth's "Day of Doom."

6. In an unpublished letter now at Yale addressed to Elisha Babcock and dated December 11, 1805, Barlow discussed the origin of the word "Keiser." Both Keiser and czar are "corruptions of the Latin Cesar, which from being a personal name became the general title of the Roman emperors."

7. Howard, p. 317.

Chapter Four

1. Zunder, p. 176.

2. Barlow sent a copy of "The Hasty Pudding" to Matthew Carey in September, 1794, shortly after the poem was written; but he was unenthusiastic about having it published. In May, 1795, he wrote to John Fellows: "As to the little poem I sent to Carey, I care nothing about it. If it should come to you, you may publish it." Woodress, p. 318. "Advice to a Raven in Russia" was first published by Lemuel G. Olmstead, Barlow's nephew, in the *Erie Chronicle* (October 10, 1843), with some errors in transcription. It was not published again until Leon Howard rediscovered it and published it in "Joel Barlow and Napoleon," *Huntingdon Library Quarterly*, II (October, 1938), 32–51. The poem is included in its entirety later in this chapter.

3. Zunder, p. 59.

4. Included in a letter now in Yale Library, J. Barlow to Major Elisha Babcock, Washington, December 11, 1805.

5. Todd, p. 292.

6. *Ibid.*, p. 293.

7. These lines are taken from a manuscript in the Yale University Library. What seems to be an earlier, slightly different version is included in Todd, p. 191, along with a letter to Robert Fulton in which Barlow described how he pasted a copy of these lines to the back of a painting of Charlotte which Fulton had done.

8. It is interesting, though perhaps presumptuous, to speculate on the relationship between the naturalness of hasty pudding and the natural goodness of man as related to the unnatural but necessary rules for preparing and consuming the meal and the equally unnatural but necessary role of government. Although Barlow apparently never had this connection in mind, one might see the poem as an allegory of his political thought. It would be wiser, however, to see both as the result of Barlow's affinity for "naturalness."

9. Van Wyck Brooks, *The World of Washington Irving* (New York, 1944), p. 59.

10. Howard, p. 295.

11. Todd, p. 281.

12. "Advice to a Raven in Russia" is published here in its entirety because it is not included in *Works*, which prints only those works published separately during Barlow's lifetime. See Leon Howard, "Joel Barlow and Napoleon," *Huntingdon Library Quarterly*, II (October, 1938), 32–51.

13. Howard, p. 295.

Chapter Five

1. Victor C. Miller, *Joel Barlow: Revolutionist, London, 1791–92* (Hamburg, 1932), p. 111.

2. Vernon Louis Parrington, *Main Currents in American Thought* (New York, 1927), I, 386.

3. Victor C. Miller has compiled a comparison of the United States Constitution, the French 1791 Constitution, Barlow's *Letter*, the French 1793 Constitution, and, on several points, the *Federalist Papers*. A chart outlining his conclusions appears following page 80 of his book.

4. Howard, p. 329.

5. Barlow's list numbers sixteen because he inadvertently skipped the number seven.

6. Howard, p. 325.

Chapter Six

1. Howard, p. 407.
2. Roy Harvey Pearce, *The Continuity of American Poetry* (Princeton, 1961), pp. 63–69.
3. Lewis Simpson, ed., *The Federalist Literary Mind* (Baton Rouge, 1962), p. 59. Simpson also includes a humorous parody of this poem by John Quincy Adams.
4. Gordon Bigelow, *Rhetoric and American Poetry of the Early National Period* (Gainesville, 1960), p. 75.
5. Woodress, p. 25.
6. Howard, p. 339.
7. Vernon Louis Parrington, ed., *The Connecticut Wits* (Hamden, Conn., 1926), p. xlviii.
8. Todd, p. 236.
9. This is taken from a manuscript in the Yale University Library. The entire letter is quoted with minor errors in transcription in Todd, pp. 295–98.
10. Todd, p. 285.

Selected Bibliography

PRIMARY SOURCES

A more detailed listing of primary source material may be found in Leon Howard, *The Connecticut Wits* (Chicago: University of Chicago Press, 1943), pp. 421–24; and Jacob Blanck, "Joel Barlow," *Bibliography of American Literature* (New Haven: Yale University Press, 1955), I, 169–84. The major holdings of Barlow papers are in the Harvard and Yale University libraries.

Advice to the Privileged Orders, in the Several States of Europe, Resulting from the Necessity and Propriety of a General Revolution in the Principle of Government. London—Printed: New York—reprinted: Childs and Swaine, ca. 1794.

"The Anarchiad—A Poem on the Restoration of Chaos and Substantial Night," *The New Haven Gazette and Connecticut Magazine.* October 26, 1786 to September 13, 1787.

The Anarchiad: A New England Poem. ed. Luther G. Riggs. New Haven: Thomas H. Pease, 1861.

The Anarchiad—A Poem on the Restoration of Chaos and Substantial Night. ed. William Bottorff. Gainesville: Scholars' Facsimiles and Reprints, 1967.

The Columbiad a Poem. Philadelphia: Fry and Kammerer: C. and A. Conrad and Co., 1807.

The Columbiad . . . With the Last Corrections of the Author . . . Paris: Printed for F. Schoell, Booksellev [*sic*], 1813.

The Columbiad. A Poem, with the Last Corrections of the Author . . . Washington City: Published by Joseph Milligan, Georgetown. June 1, 1825.

The Conspiracy of Kings. London: J. Johnson, St. Paul's Church Yard, 1792.

An Elegy on the Late Honorable Titus Hosmer, Esq; One of the Counsellors of the State of Connecticut, a Member of Congress, and a Judge of the Maritime Court of Appeals for the United States of America. Hartford: Printed by Hudson & Goodwin, [n.d., 1782].

The Hasty Pudding: A Poem, in Three Cantos. Written at Chambery, in Savoy, January, 1793. New Haven: [n.p.], 1796.

Letters from Paris, to the Citizens of the United States of America, on the System of Policy Hitherto Pursued by Their Government Relative to their Commercial Intercourse with England and France, etc. London: Printed for James Ridgway, York Street, St. James's Square, by A. Wilson, Wild Court, 1800.

Letter to Henry Gregoire, Bishop, Senator, Compte of the Empire and Member of the Institute of France, in Reply to His Letter on the Columbiad. Washington City: Printed by Roger Chew Weightman, 1809.

A Letter to the National Convention of France, on the Defects in the Constitution of 1791, and the Extent of the Amendments Which Ought to be Applied. To Which is Added the Conspiracy of Kings, a Poem. New York: Printed by Thomas Greenleaf, for J. Fellows, No. 192, Water Street, [n.d., ca. 1793].

A Letter, Addressed to the People of Piedmont, on the Advantages of the French Revolution, and the Necessity of Adopting Its Principles in Italy . . . Translated From the French by the Author. London: Printed by Daniel Isaac Eaton, 1795.

An Oration, Delivered at the North Church in Hartford, at the Meeting of the Connecticut Society of the Cincinnati, July 4th, 1787. In Commemoration of the Independence of the United States. Hartford: Printed by Hudson and Goodwin, Near the Bridge, [1787].

Oration Delivered at Washington, July Fourth, 1809; at the Request of the Democratic Citizens of the District of Columbia. Washington City: Printed and Published by R. C. Weightman, 1809.

A Poem, Spoken at the Public Commencement at Yale College, in New-Haven; September 12, 1781. Hartford: Printed by Hudson & Goodwin, [1781].

The Political Writings of Joel Barlow. Containing Advice to the Privileged Orders. Letter to the National Convention. Letter to the People of Piedmont. The Conspiracy of Kings. A New Edition Corrected. Printed at New-York, by Mott & Lyon, for Fellows & Adam, Thomas Greenleaf, and Naphtali Judah, 1796.

The Prospect of Peace. A Poetical Composition, Delivered in Yale-College, at the Public Examination, of the Candidates for the Degree of Bachelor of Arts; July 23, 1778. New-Haven: Printed by Thomas and Samuel Green, 1778.

Prospectus of a National Institution, to be Established in the United States. Washington City: Printed by Samuel H. Smith, 1806.

A Review of Robert Smith's Address to the People of the United States. Originally Published in the National Intelligencer. Philadelphia: John Binns, 1811.

The Vision of Columbus; a Poem in Nine Books. Hartford: Printed by Hudson and Goodwin, for the Author, 1787.

The Vision of Columbus . . . the Fifth Edition, Corrected . . . to Which is Added, The Conspiracy of Kings. Paris: Printed at the English Press, 1793.

Bottorff, William and Arthur Ford (eds.). *The Works of Joel Barlow.* 2 vols. Gainesville: Scholars' Facsimiles and Reprints, 1970.

Cantor, Milton. "A Connecticut Yankee in a Barbary Court: Joel Barlow's Algerian Letters to His Wife," *William and Mary Quarterly*, XIX (January, 1962), 86–109.

Howard, Leon. "Joel Barlow and Napoleon," *Huntingdon Library Quarterly*, II (October, 1938), 32–51. Contains "Advice to a Raven in Russia."

Zunder, Theodore. "A New Barlow Poem," *American Literature*, XI (May, 1939), 206–9.

SECONDARY SOURCES

Adams, M. Ray. "Joel Barlow, Political Romanticist," *American Literature*, IX (May, 1937), 113–52. Account of Barlow's stay in Europe with emphasis on his prose writings.

––––––. "On the 'Newly Discovered Letter' of Joel Barlow," *American Literature*, X (May, 1938), 224–27. Challenges the accuracy of Maxfield's designation of "newly discovered" to Barlow's letter to his wife from Algiers.

Ball, Kenneth R. "A Great Society: The Social and Political Thought of Joel Barlow." Ph.D. dissertation, University of Wisconsin, 1967. Traces Barlow's emerging political utopianism.

––––––. "Joel Barlow's 'Canal' and Natural Religion," *Eighteenth Century Studies*, II (Spring, 1969), 225–39. Demonstrates connection between Barlow's developing "natural religion" as seen in "The Canal" (published here for the first time) and as seen in his translation of Volney's *Ruins.*

Beers, H. A. *The Connecticut Wits and Other Essays.* New Haven: Yale University Press, 1920. One introductory essay on the Wits.

Bigelow, Gordon. *Rhetoric and American Poetry of the Early National Period.* Gainesville: University of Florida Press, 1960. Discussion of American poetry between 1775 and 1815 in terms of various modes of discourse, including Classical.

Blau, Joseph L. "Joel Barlow, Enlightened Religionist," *Journal of History of Ideas*, X (June, 1949), 430–44. Traces Barlow's criticism of church orthodoxy and hierarchy through his poetry and prose, seeing this position as typical of enlightened thinkers of the time.

Boynton, P. H. "Joel Barlow Advises the Privileged Orders," *New England Quarterly*, XII (September, 1939), 477–99. Examination of *Advice* and of the forces working on Barlow at the time he was writing it.

Brant, Irving. "Joel Barlow, Madison's Stubborn Minister," *William and Mary Quarterly*, XV (October, 1958), 438–51. Examination of Barlow's final mission to France with emphasis on the persistence with which he pursued it.

Bridgwater, Dorothy W. "The Barlow Manuscripts in the Yale Library," *Yale University Library Gazette,* XXXIV (October, 1959), 57–63. Includes texts of five letters.

Brooks, Van Wyck. *The World of Washington Irving.* New York: E. P. Dutton & Co., Inc., 1944.

Cantor, Milton. "Joel Barlow: Lawyer and Legal Philosopher," *American Quarterly*, X (Summer, 1958), 165–74. A discussion of Barlow's dissertation for admission to the bar.

––––––. "The Life of Joel Barlow." Ph.D. dissertation, Columbia University, 1964. Examination of Barlow's political philosophy with special emphasis on his prose.

Christensen, Merton A. "Deism in Joel Barlow's Early Work: Heterodox Passages in *The Vision of Columbus*," *American Literature*, XXVII (January, 1956), 509–20. Sees certain passages in the 1787 *Vision* that reflect ideas associated with eighteenth-century Deism.

Davis, J. S. *Essays in the Earlier History of American Corporations.* Cambridge: Harvard University Press, 1917, I, 124–50, 213–53. Account of the Scioto Associates.

Dorfman, Joseph. "Joel Barlow: Trafficker in Trade and Letters," *Political Science Quarterly*, LIX (March, 1944), 83–100. Describes Barlow's business ventures, especially on the Continent.

Dos Passos, John. *The Ground We Stand On.* New York: Har-court, Brace, and Co., 1941. Praise of Barlow's democratic political philosophy.

Durden, Robert F. "Joel Barlow in the French Revolution," *William and Mary Quarterly*, VIII (July, 1951), 327–54. Account of Barlow's affairs in France during 1792–94.

Erdman, David V. "William Blake's Debt to Joel Barlow," *American Literature*, XXVI (March, 1954), 94–98. Suggests that Blake may have used portions of Book Five of the 1787 edition of *The Vision of Columbus* as a source for his poem "America: A Prophecy."

Greider, Theodore. "Joel Barlow's *The Hasty Pudding*: A Study in American Neo-Classicism," *British Association for American Studies Bulletin* (December, 1965), 35–42. Examines Barlow's most famous poem within the context of eighteenth-century poetry.

Howard, Leon. *The Connecticut Wits.* Chicago: University of Chicago Press, 1943. Excellent treatment of Barlow, John Trumbull, Timothy Dwight, and David Humphries. Especially for intellectual, philosophical, and esthetic currents during the period.

————. "The Late Eighteenth Century: An Age of Contradictions," *Transitions in American Literary History.* Ed. Harry Hayden Clark. Durham: Octagon Books, 1954. Emphasis on crosscurrents of thought during this period.

————. "Joel Barlow and Napoleon," *Huntingdon Library Quarterly*, II (October, 1938), 37–51. Account of Barlow's Russian journey.

————. *The Vision of Joel Barlow.* Los Angeles: The Grey Bow Press, 1937. Brief, privately printed account of life and contribution.

Leary, Lewis. "Joel Barlow and William Hayley," *American Literature*, XXI (November, 1949), 325–34. Discussion of correspondence between these two men during Barlow's residency in England, 1791–92.

Maxfield, Ezra K. "A Newly Discovered Letter from Joel Barlow to His Wife, from Algiers," *American Literature*, IX (January, 1938), 442–49. Printing of a manuscript from Barlow to his wife, Ruth.

————. "The Tom Barlow Manuscript of the *Columbiad.*" *New England Quarterly*, XI (December, 1938), 834–42. Argues that this manuscript is the original revision for *The Columbiad.*

—————. "To the Editors of American Literature," *American Literature*, X (November, 1938), 351–52. Answers an attack by M. Ray Adams on the authenticity of a manuscript copy of Barlow's letter to his wife from Algiers.

McGuire, Mabelle B. "Barlow, Man of Freedom," *The Personalist*, XLII (Spring, 1961), 203–6. Brief account of some highlights of Barlow's life with emphasis on his concern for freedom.

Miller, Victor C. *Joel Barlow: Revolutionist, London, 1791–1792.* Hamburg: Friederichsen, de Gruyter & Co., 1932. Extensive use of documents in British archives for an account of Barlow's activities during this period.

Parrington, Vernon Louis, ed. *The Connecticut Wits.* Hamden, Conn.: Archon, 1926. Anthology and introduction still valuable.

—————. *Main Currents in American Thought.* 3 vols. New York: Harcourt, Brace, and Co., 1927–30.

Pearce, Roy Harvey. *The Continuity of American Poetry.* Princeton: Princeton University Press, 1961. Discussion of *The Columbiad* in the tradition of the American epic.

—————. "Toward an American Epic," *Hudson Review*, XII (Autumn, 1959), 362–77. Discussion of Barlow, Whitman, and Pound.

Simpson, Lewis P., ed. *The Federalist Literary Mind.* Baton Rouge: Louisiana State University Press, 1962. Anthology of the National period.

Spencer, Benjamin T. *The Quest for Nationality.* Syracuse: Syracuse University Press, 1957. Theme of American literary independence traced through the history of American literature.

Todd, Charles B. *Life and Letters of Joel Barlow.* New York: G. P. Putnam, 1886. Early biography containing many letters and other manuscript material; not always accurate in transcription.

Tyler, Moses Coit. *Three Men of Letters.* New York: G. P. Putnam, 1895. Contains one essay on Barlow.

Woodress, James. *A Yankee's Odyssey: The Life of Joel Barlow.* Philadelphia, J. B. Lippincott Company, 1958. The standard life.

Zunder, Theodore. *The Early Days of Joel Barlow.* New Haven: Yale University Press, 1934. Detailed biography to 1787.

Index

Adams, John, 35
Addison, Joseph, 24
Virgil, *Aeneid*, 64, 74
Alsop, Richard, 36
American Mercury, 21, 26, 86
Arnold, Benedict, 19
Atlas, 82

Babcock, Elisha, 20, 21, 86
Bacon, Francis, 120
Baldwin, Abraham, 20, 35, 36
Baldwin, Clara, 42, 102
Baldwin, Michael, 20
Baldwin, Ruth (Mrs. Joel Barlow), 19, 28-29, 30, 31, 32, 33, 34, 35, 37, 38, 40, 41, 42, 43, 44, 48, 85, 102, 130
Barbary Pirates, 33-34
Barlow, Joel: birth, 13; business enterprises, 27-29, 33; Chaplaincy, 19-20; death, 45, 106, 130; departure for France, 27; diplomacy in Algiers, 34; education, 13-18; elder statesman, 39-43; lawyer, 22; life at Kalorama, 39; marriage, 20; Minister to France, 43-45, 102, 121; printer and publisher, 20-22; politician, 31-32, 94-95; reputation, 126-28; return to the United States, 38; teaching, 18

WRITINGS:

"Advice to a Raven in Russia," 45, 85, 102-6, 126
Advice to the Privileged Orders, 29-30, 109-13, 118
Anarchiad, The, 22-24, 29

"Blest Hymen, Hail That Memorable Day," 87
"Canal, The, 37
Columbiad, The, 19, 32, 39, 40-41, 48, 59, 68, 69, 72, 73, 74-84, 85, 96, 98, 124, 125, 126
Conspiracy of Kings, The, 30
"Could Youth, Could Innocence, Could Beauty Save," 87
Hasty Pudding, The, 32, 85, 86, 94-102, 126
Letters from Paris, 35-36, 117-19, 121, 126
Letter to Henry Gregoire, 124-25
Letter to the National Convention of France, A, 30-31, 113-15
Letter, Addressed to the People of Piedmont, A, 32, 113-16
"New Year's Poem for 1806," 86
"On the Discoveries of Captain Lewis," 127
Oration, Delivered at the North Church in Hartford, An, 122
Oration Delivered at Washington, 42-43, 121-22, 127
Poem, Spoken at the Public Commencement at Yale College, A, 87, 89-94
Political Writings of Joel Barlow, The, 32
Prospect of Peace, The, 17, 87-89
Prospectus of a National Institution, 39-40, 119-21
Review of Robert Smith's Address, A, 123
Vision of Columbus, The, 18,

19, 20, 21, 25, 30, 32, 37, 38, 39, 40, 46-67, 68, 71, 72, 73, 74, 78, 84, 85, 88, 89, 90, 91, 96, 100, 119, 126
Vision of Columbus, The (Fifth Edition), 68-74, 84
Volney's *Ruins* (trans.), 119
Watts's *Psalms* (trans.), 21
Barlow, Samuel (father of Joel Barlow), 13
Barlow, Thomas (nephew of Joel Barlow), 44, 45, 102
Beattie, James, *Elements of Criticism*, 63
Bigelow, Gordon, quoted, 127
Bovadilla, Francis de, 48
Brooks, Van Wyck, quoted, 102
Buckminster, Joseph, 15, 18, 19
Burgoyne, General John, 58
Burke, Edmund, 94, 112; *Reflections on the Revolution in France*, 29, 109

Cain and Abel, 19
Cavalier Poetry, 16, 85, 87
Cheetham, James, 128-29
Columbus, Christopher, 47, 48, 49, 50, 52, 59, 60, 61, 67, 78, 90, 91
Connecticut Wits, 19, 20, 23-24, 36, 59, 68, 122, 128
Constitution Society, 30, 31
Copley, John Singleton, 59
Cortez, 51
Cornwallis, General Charles, 58
Cyrus the Great, 19

Dagget, Naphtali, 17
Daniel, 19
Dante, 106
Dartmouth College, 14, 59
Deism, 18, 23, 47, 55, 70, 71, 123
Dwight, Timothy, 18, 20, 23, 46, 59

Ecrilla, Don Alonzo de, *Araucana*, 64
Edinburgh Review, 41

Edwards, Jonathan, *Inquiry Into the Freedom of the Will*, 14
Erasmus, 56

Franklin, Benjamin, 25, 58, 59
Freneau, Philip, 85
Fulton, Robert, 37, 40, 41, 42, 43, 121

Godfrey, Thomas, 59
Goethe, Johann Wolfgang von, 84
Gregoire, Henry, 124-25
Gustavus III, King of Sweden, 30

Hamilton, Alexander, 25, 31
Hartford Courant, 36
Hesper, 74
Homer, *Odyssey*, 74; *Iliad*, 64, 74
Hopkins, Lemuel, 22
Hosmer, Titus, 58
Howard, Leon, 72, 84, 124, 126; quoted, 14, 24, 25, 43, 63, 68, 102, 106, 120, 128
Humphreys, David, 19, 20, 22, 25, 33, 60

Jefferson, Thomas, 27, 35, 36, 38, 40, 41, 68, 119
Johnson, Joseph, 29
Joseph, 19

Kames, Lord, *Elements of Criticism*, 14-15, 63
Kibly, Charles, 26

Lafayette, Marquis de, 25, 27
Laud, Archbishop, 57
Leopold, King of Austria, 30
Lewis, Merriwether, 42, 127
London Monthly Magazine, 41
Louis the Sixteenth, 25, 29, 30, 72, 73
Loyola, 56
Lucan, 75
Lucinda and Heartly, 74, 80-82
Luther, Martin, 56
Lycon, Matthew, 35-36
Lycurgus, 54

Madison, James, 31, 41, 43, 123
Mahomet, 54
Manco Capac, 47, 52-55
Marmontel, Juan Francisco, *The Incas: or the Destruction of the Battle of Peru*, 64
Meigs, Josiah, 18, 41
Milton, John, 127; *Paradise Lost*, 64, 78
Monroe, James, 32, 33, 34, 35, 43, 68
Montezuma, 51
Moor's Indian School, 13
Moses, 54

Napoleon, 43, 44, 45, 85, 102, 103, 105, 106, 116, 121
National Convention, 95, 124
Nemours, DuPont de, 120
New Haven Gazette and Connecticut Magazine, The, 22, 25

Ohio Company, 27
Ovando, Nicholas de, 48

Paine, Thomas, 25, 27, 29, 31, 32, 113, 128, 129; *The Rights of Man*, 29, 109
Parrington, Vernon Louis, quoted, 113, 128
Pearce, Roy Harvey, 126
Penn, William, 57
Peter of Russia, 54
Philadelphia Portfolio, 41
Pinckney, Charles, 35
Pizarro, 55
Pope, Alexander, 16, 24, 27, 64, 65, 82; *The Dunciad*, 20
Potowmac, 74, 82
Price, Richard, 29
Priestley, Joseph 29

Queen Isabella, 48

Raleigh, Sir Walter, 56
Randolph, John, 58
Riggs, Luther G., 23
Rittenhouse, David, 59

Robertson, William, *The History of America*, 64
Robespierre, 32
Rousseau, Jean-Jacques, 15
Rush, Benjamin, 120

Scioto Associates, 27, 28, 33
Shays's Rebellion, 22
Shipman, Elias, 26
Smith, Robert, 123
Spencer, Benjamin T., *The Quest for Nationality*, 63
Steele, Richard, 24
Sullivan, James, 120
Swift, Jonathan, 24

Trumbull, John (the painter), 59
Trumbull, John (the poet), 18, 20, 22, 59

Valverde, Father Vincent, 55
Vega, Garcilaso de la, *The Royal Commentaries of Peru*, 64
Villett, Charlotte, 87
Voltaire, Jean, *Candide*, 60; *Essay on Epic Poetry*, 64

Washington, George, 16, 19, 25, 31, 36, 57, 58, 64, 67, 80, 98, 117
Webster, Noah, 18, 20, 21, 36, 40, 83
West, Benjamin, 59
Whitman, Walt, *Leaves of Grass*, 24, 127
Williams, William Carlos, *Paterson*, 126
Wolcott, Oliver, 13, 18
Woodress, James, 65, 67, 68; quoted, 14, 26, 30, 32, 128
Wollstonecraft, Mary, 29

XYZ Affair, 35

Yale University, 14, 46, 59, 87, 88, 89

Zunder, Theodore, quoted, 85